The Last Resort For Livelihood

A Study of People who Beg

Bachitter Singh

Published and Printed By:

CreateSpace Independent Publishing Platform

An Amazon Company

Scotts Valley, California

www.createspace.com / www.amazon.com

ISBN-10: **1976534461**
ISBN-13: **978-1976534461**

In the Reminiscence of my Dad,

Whose advice and ideals will always

remain alive with me.

CONTENTS

ACKNOWLEDGMENTS

This book is an edited version of Research work that I conducted during my M.Phil. It is a delight to acknowledge here the important contributions that many people have made over the past few years which allowed me reach where I am today.

I take this opportunity to express my deep sense of gratitude and profound reverence to my esteemed supervisor, Dr. Hema Gandotra, Assistant Professor, Department of Sociology, University of Jammu, under whose able guidance and supervision I took this task and gave it present shape. I sincerely appreciate her constant involvement, pain-taking efforts and affectionate nature. Her advice and suggestions are unforgettable. It was a privilege and honour to work with her. Without her constant supervision, it would not have been possible to complete the work. This research could not be possible without the help of my esteemed supervisor, Dr. Hema Gandotra.

I am thankful to the Head of the Department, Dr. Vishav Raksha (present) and Prof. Abha Chauhan (former), who have always encouraged, inspired and supported me with their important and much needed suggestions. Their inputs helped me immensely during my research work.

I would also like to express my sincere gratitude to other faculty members of our department, Dr. Sapna Sangra for her valuable help and suggestions during my research work.

I am highly indebted and obliged to the non-teaching staff of department of Sociology, all my senior scholars and friends for their help and cooperation during my M.Phil. course.

Special thanks to the respondents of my study. I would like to express my deepest gratitude to all those who have participated in the present research, directly and indirectly. I would like to thank them for sparing their time and sharing their life stories and experiences which has helped me to shape my M.Phil. work in the present form.

Special thanks to Mr. Chail Singh (my Nephew) and Mr. Rajesh Kumar Bhandari (Friend) who have assisted me a few times, in the field during my research.

Apart from this I am also thankful to my family for providing me support and encouragement which inspires always, to do better in life. Special reverence and deepest gratitude to my DAD (who is no more with us now), Late Sh. Ram Lal Manhas, who had always encouraged me, inspired me and taught me how to remain firm in difficult times. I am also thankful to my mother, Smt. Anshru Devi and to my wife Ms. Pinkee Manhas for providing me support and encouragement throughout the research. My sweet little angel, Nitibha Manhas (daughter) relieved me from all the burdens and pains just with her one smile. Though, I could not have managed to give her ample time, but she remained a source of inspiration and contentment for me, with her cute face.

Finally, my sincere thanks to all those who extended their help in word and deed, in one way or the other in accomplishment of this task.

Bachitter Singh

1: INTRODUCTION

"Like you don't really plan ahead. You just think of the day. You live for the day. See yourself all right. Stop yourself from rattling.... But like it's better begging than going out and mugging old grannies and robbing houses and that, and shoplifting, definitely." - A Beggar's account quoted by Dean & Melrose (1999)[1]

In every society everyone - men or women, children or old, fit or disabled have to engage themselves in some kind of work[*] or some activity for their livelihood and to survive; and those who can/do not do anything must have a person, group or institution – usually family member, relative, friend or some charity organisation or even welfare state, on whom they can be dependent on (Gore, 1958).[2] This is the base of not just the economic system but also of the social structure and culture of a society as one's work determines one's status (achieved) and corresponding role in a particular society; and in turn society (culture,

---

[*] Work is the creation of material goods or services, which may be directly consumed by the worker or sold to someone else. Work thus includes not only paid labour but also self-employed labour and unpaid labour, including production of goods and services done in the home (Hodson & Sullivan, The Social Organization of Work, 2008). Sociology emphasize the centrality of work, per se, to individual well-being (Gill, 1999).

norms and values) influences individual's response to work and dependence. As Hughes[3] states that "a man's work is as good a clue as any, to the course of his life, and to his social being and identity." Society through its various institutions and agencies encourages or motivates its members to engage themselves in some productive work[†] in order to survive and to prosper [like 'Goal Attainment' in Parsons (1951)[4] AGIL model] and also to support their dependents especially their family members. Despite this motivation by society, there could arise some complicated situations like what if a person who is incapable of doing any work and have no one to support him? Or any other situation in which an individual does not or could not conform to the social norm of doing some productive work? In this situation, when individuals can/do not engage in any productive work, they most likely engage themselves in any alternate (or informal or even illegal) economic activity for livelihood which may or may not be encouraged by larger society. Begging is one such alternate economic activity although it can be described as work, when viewed from beggars' perspective. Shichor and Ellis (1981)[5] in their study asserted that "all the beggars, referred to begging as their work and most of them claimed that they were the main breadwinners and the heads of their families". Dean (1999)[6] observed that a number of beggar participants (in his study) referred to begging as a 'job' or as 'work', or to their takings as 'earnings'. He further asserted that some beggar participants even referred to the passers-by who gave them money as their 'customers' and stressed the importance of both affording 'respect' to their customers and winning it from them in return.

"I work every day. I can't stand sitting at home.... Tell you what, it's a job, it's a job. I'm telling you, there's as many ins and outs involved in begging and busking and street working as there is in any other job. Probably more in fact. Some people say 'Get yourself a job!', but I always tell them that they should try it themselves ... it can be a very distressing job." – A Beggar's account as quoted by Dean (1999)

Shichor & Ellis (1981),[7] argued that some literatures and theorists for example Arnold (2008) have also characterized some begging as a form

---

[†]   Sanctioned by society and directly or indirectly (like household work) economically profitable. Productive work is used interchangeably with work.

of work, one with elements of artistry and skill acquired through exercise, experiences and observation of role models. Begging involves the expenditure of effort and skill in order to obtain an income in money or goods, and hence it can be described as 'work', yet it produces no material output (goods) and no clearly definable service. Begging can be perceived as a Deviant Occupation or work. As Polsky (1969),[8] argued that an occupation can be perceived as deviant if it has any of the following characteristics:

a) It is "illegal";

b) It violates "what is considered morally correct behaviour towards one's fellow men";

c) It is not considered to be "a proper or fitting occupation" by society.

In India, begging is illegal as per various anti-begging laws and also not considered proper or fitting occupation by society so it clearly fits into Polsky's Deviant occupation category. However as per Census of India (in categorisation of workers, marginal workers and non- workers), begging is not recognised as work or occupation and beggars are categorised as 'Non-Workers'[‡] in census data.

The present Book has explored the socio-cultural and economic life of the beggars (persons engaged in begging) in Jammu city. The study has looked into the deplorable conditions of the beggars in the city and has explored the reasons and causes of begging. The study also focused on the interaction process between the beggars and the society.

The beggar population is not a homogeneous one. It includes people from different religions, caste, ethnicity, regions, and cultures. The only parameter which categorise them as one group is their economic activity i.e., begging. However, one can find various similarities among these different groups or individuals due to their similar economic activity. So, due to their (beggars') similar economic condition, they have somewhat similar ideologies, housing patterns and life-styles and so on. Many research studies suggested that most of the beggars do not have proper houses to live (Dean, 1999).[9] They are either homeless or live in sub-

---

[‡] 'Non workers' are defined in the Census as individuals who do not participate in any economic activity – paid or unpaid – household duties, or cultivation.

standard (like *Jhuggis* in Indian scenario) shelters. Due to lack of a home, they usually remain in unhygienic lifestyle and also due to their occupation's (Begging) prerequisite. The present study has explored the socio-cultural and economic profile of beggars, by taking into consideration various parameters like - their family and marriage institution, education, economy, house/shelter and food patterns etc.

As begging is seen as a deviant and at many places an illegal activity, so the question arises, why people beg? Various studies addressed this question and come up with possible causes of begging. These studies suggested that the phenomenon of begging is a result of a number of factors, such as poverty, religion, physical disability, culture, bad habits (drug, alcohol, and gambling etc.), family heritage, uncontrolled rural to urban migration, and psychiatric disabilities and disorders, etc. In the absence of any means of livelihood, a large number of people were driven to begging, some temporarily and some permanently. Mukharjee (1945),[10] had pointed out that beggary is a symptom of social disorganization and the widespread custom of alms-giving by individuals and institutions by which the disability, helplessness or social inadequacy of the beggars has been sought to be mitigated in India. He argued that the most frequent cause of beggary is the increasing proportions of population by which workers displaced from the land and unable to find employment or subsistence but in addition to this displaced worker, there are the physically handicapped, the blind, the deaf-mutes, etc. who also take to begging.

Tara Patel (1959),[11] in a study in Ahamedabad summarised the reasons of begging as: i) Poverty, Unsupported, unemployed, part-time beggars ii) Habitual Beggars iii) Physically handicapped, mentally retarded, diseased iv) Cruelty of relatives v) To live a care free life vi) Fatalist vii) Shameful remorse for his incestuous relation viii) Helped to live as prostitute.

B.B. Pande (1986)[12] argued that social parasitism (begging) is inspired by any of three motivations: i) by economic necessity resulting from extreme resourcelessness and destitution; ii) by the altruistic spirit based on religious or traditional considerations as in the case of *sadhu, sanyasi, darvesh* and *fakir*, and iii) hedonistic considerations designed to avoid the drudgery of hard work and industry.

Anderson (1961)[13] has classified causes of begging into unemployment and seasonal work; the misfits of industry; defects of personality; crisis in the life of the person; racial or national discrimination and wanderlust. The present study has also highlighted and discussed different reasons and causes of begging and found some major causes as poverty, unemployment, illiteracy, hereditary occupation, encouragement by religion, pity for vulnerable, easy money etc. which are almost identical to the causes mentioned in various other studies.

Begging activity could not be understood in isolation as an individual problem but as a pattern of repetitive interactions between a beggar and society. Gore (1958),[14] is of the view that in earlier studies on the beggar 'problem' the focus of analysis has been the beggar himself, his mind, his attitudes, his handicap, his satisfaction, dissatisfaction, etc. He argued that such a mode of analysis is fallacious and misleading. It is fallacious because it loses sight of the fact that begging as a pattern of behaviour cannot be understood except as a process of interaction between the beggar and the giver. Begging requires the acquiescence of the members of the larger society. As begging is a repetitive pattern of behaviour, it can be understood only as a process of interaction between two more or less institutionalized roles, that of the beggar and that of the giver. The beggar stretches out a hand and expresses a 'need' toward which the giver's action is oriented. The giver meets this 'need' by dropping a coin in the outstretched hand of the beggar: in meeting the need of the beggar in this particular way he is acting in accordance with certain 'norms' characteristic of his group and is simultaneously re-enforcing the beggar's particular pattern of meeting his need. He further tried to explain begging as consisting of three interrelated acts of Begging, Giving and Receiving and attitude of society to each of them varies greatly. This is so not only in our society, but in all societies. Giving is encouraged, and begging is discouraged. Yet if there were no begging, there would be no need for giving - at least in the present restricted sense where giving is by definition oriented to the needs of a particular person and not to the impersonal needs of an institution. Gore (1958), further argues that the attitude of society to a person who asks for alms, but is not a religious mendicant is different. As a beggar, he claims one's sympathy but not one's respect. Begging itself is a misfortune. No person would beg unless he had to. But then-in the context of the Karma philosophy-no person can disclaim total responsibility even for his misfortunes. And, therefore, there is a sense of shame attached to begging. The beggar experiences a loss of social status, even if his begging is due to factors entirely beyond his control.

Beggars use different techniques to get alms like fortune telling, women tow dirty children behind them, pleading with pedestrians, unwanted services (like cleaning glasses of vehicles or selling flowers on signal), sitting on pavements, stretching hands or bowls, and using religious ethos. In some particular seasons or festivals, the number of beggars increases like, during the Amarnath Yatra period and on the eve of different festivals like Eid, Diwali, Shivratri, Gurpurab, Navratras etc.[15] This mainly happens because during this period there is more rush of people in markets and religious places (and also they are in celebration mood), as a result beggars get more alms. The present study has explored the encounters of beggars and society, mainly focused on religious perspective on alms giving, views of people on begging and beggars, and techniques used by beggars while begging.

Dean (1999),[16] sees the existence of contemporary begging as failure of welfare state. The phenomenon of begging depicts social inequality and exclusion. Welfare state which is supposed to uplift the marginalised, socially excluded and economically downtrodden classes of people have ignored this section of people (beggars) as they are mainly powerless due to lack of any political lobbying for them. Governments and political parties always claims, they will work for the poor, especially during the time of elections. But the poorest among poor i.e., beggars have yet to receive the attention of government. Instead of welfare measures for them, government have criminalised begging (their only source of livelihood), by anti-begging laws. In majority of Indian states (presently 20 states and 2 union Territories including Jammu and Kashmir) begging is a criminal offence in accordance with Bombay Prevention of Begging Act (1959) which was later extended to the other states and union territories. Under this law, officials of the Social Welfare Department assisted by the police, conduct raids to pick up beggars who they then try in special courts called 'beggar courts'. If convicted, they are sent to certified institutions called 'beggar homes' (these beggar homes exists in only seven states and one union territory) also known as *'Sewa Kutir'* for a period ranging from one to ten years for detention, training and employment. However, as Dean (1999) argues that in reality, many people found begging, are not prosecuted. The present study has also explored the legal perspective on begging and various other problems faced by beggars in their daily life like harassment from public, competition among beggars themselves, homelessness, etc.

The basic contradiction in begging as an economic activity is that, an individual (poor or fraud) engaged in this activity can earn money or alms without providing any goods and services in exchange, which is against the modern capitalistic societies. The begging is, thus, an informal, alternate and at many places illegal (as per anti-begging laws, although these laws are not enforced most of the times) economic activity, but, it is a life saviour for the destitute, disabled and others who are otherwise unfit, rejected or simply have no interest in race of life (social system) in modern competitive societies.

BEGGING

Begging is a form of street-level economic activity. Begging is the practice or an economic activity whereby a person obtains money, food or other things from people they encounter by request without the intention of returning. Begging is an ancient, widespread and enigmatic (controversial) occupation (Bromley, 1981).[17] Although varying by geography and the times, begging is universal. People who beg are among the most vulnerable in society, often trapped in poverty and deprivation, and it is regarded as a risky and demeaning activity (Dean, 1999).[18]

According to Dean (1999) begging refers to "the unlawful solicitation of a voluntary unilateral gift in a public place".

According to the *International Labour Organization* (2004)[19] begging is defined as: "a range of activities whereby an individual asks a stranger for money on the basis of being poor or needing charitable donations for health or religious reasons. Beggars may also sell small items, such as dusters or flowers, in return for money that may have little to do with the value of the item for sale".

According to Bombay Prevention of begging act 1959 "Begging" means:

(a)   Soliciting or receiving alms, in a public place whether or not under any pretence such as singing, dancing, fortune telling, performing or offering any article for sale;

(b)   entering on any private premises for the purpose of soliciting or receiving alms;

(c)   exposing or exhibiting, with the object of obtaining or extorting alms, any sore, wound injury, deformity of diseases whether of a human being or animal;

(d)   having no visible means of subsistence and wandering, about or remaining in any public place in such condition or manner, as makes it likely that the person doing so exist soliciting or receiving alms;

(e)   allowing oneself to be used as an exhibit for the purpose of soliciting or receiving alms; but does not include soliciting or receiving money or food or given for a purpose authorizes by any law.

However, the present study has focused on only those beggars who just solicit for alms (money and food items) and do not sell any article.

Begging is a multifaceted phenomenon, some see it as blessing while others as curse. Some of the connotations or views on begging, according to different thinkers and studies are as follows:

- Begging is an economic activity of destitute, disabled (physically or mentally) and other similar individuals. Individuals with extreme poverty, isolation or disability; have none to take care of them and no or very little support from state (or other organisation) find it very difficult to sustain life. Begging provides them the financial support they need. If they would not have started begging they could have died by now. When they were in dire need of money (before they started begging) nobody has offered them any help, so nobody should try to restraint them (Dean, 1999).[20]

- Begging is the last resort for livelihood (Bardach & Patashnik, 2006).[21] No one wants to beg if given a chance to choose among different occupations. Individuals who have tried to earn through different other means and failed or could not get a chance to do other things are left with no option but to beg from others. This view of begging depicts that beggars are like normal human beings who are forced by circumstances (primarily by unemployment and poverty) into begging. Many others who were trapped in similar situations may turn to theft, drug dealing, crimes, prostitutions etc. which are much worse than begging.

- Begging is a culture of some poor individuals or groups. In many individuals and groups poverty perpetuates as a culture from generation to generation (Lewis, 1998).[22] They could have overcome the poverty if they would work hard but due to the force of their culture (somewhat like Caste system) they remain less motivated and unable (or sometime don't want) to change their situation. Begging is not only an economic activity, it becomes a culture, a culture of poverty. In this scenario begging as an occupation/culture passes from generation to generation with the tool of socialisation. It is true for some groups/caste, for whom begging is their traditional caste occupation.

- Begging is becoming occupation of lazy and fraud people (it is a general perception among common people and also spreaded by *masala* media). Advocates of this view (which are majority) argue that there are so many young able-bodied men, women and children in begging who could do any other productive work. They are in begging because they are frauds and lazy. Begging don't need educational qualification, skill, hard work, or pain (physical or mental). Those lazy people who don't want to do hard work (like labour work) simply go for begging. Some may pose themselves as religious mendicant, sick, weak, or in extreme need of money to earn money (Puri 2015).[23]

- Begging is a social problem which causes public nuisance. Beggars usually roam around public place where they can find more people together. They may disturb the passer-by, irritate them or even intimidate them. Beggars interferes the privacy of other individuals and thus are seen as agents of causing public nuisance. They put the passer-by in moral/ethical dilemma, even refusing them may result in a feeling of guilt or confusion for people/passer-by (Stones, 2013).[24]

- Beggars are unidentified persons and migrants posing security threat. The attraction of the activity of begging is that it does not require any identification of people who are engaged in it. When unidentified persons are roaming freely and migrating from place to places, they pose a security threat to the local residents (Frink, 2010).[25]

- There is a buzz among general public (laymen, professionals and even among the intellectuals) about begging that begging is an activity organised, controlled and propagated by some mafia or gangs. Tara Patel (1959)[26] argued that sometimes children are made disabled by the professionals or at times some parents make use of their defective children to create sympathy amongst the alms-givers. Although in her study only one case of forced disability was found, that was of a young boy who said that he was made blind by his owner who forced him to beg.

Begging Categories

Horn and Cooke (2011)[27] have proposed three different categories of begging behaviour:

- *Passive begging* techniques refer to those individuals who either sit or stand in one spot with a sign alerting passers-by that they need money. It is also possible to include an extended hand towards passers-by as a passive begging technique.

- *Active begging* techniques refer to individuals who follow passers-by and ask for money, but who are easily put off when refused. They do not employ any forms of stand-over tactics.

- *Aggressive begging* techniques refer to obtaining money from members of the public by using stand-over tactics and threatening speech or behaviour. Aggressive techniques elicit fear and discomfort and often border on criminal assault.

One find these categories in context of present study, although, the aggressive begging is less prevalent here.

BEGGARS

A documentary on begging by Al Jazeera English TV Channel (Phillips & Shah, 2016)[28] introduced beggars with these lines, "They are the poorest of the poor and you can find them all over the world, in the wealthiest part of the West and in the Asia's poorest slums. Nobody is too young to beg; a small boy of 5 years is at the traffic signal a place where rich meet the poor..."

Beggars are the persons who solicit money (by begging) from other people without the intention of returning, or simply the individuals engaged in begging. Beggars are known by different names in different places, time and context, like - Panhandlers, Vagabonds, Mendicants, Vagrants, Tramps, Bums[§] (although each of them is slightly different from others) etc.

Beggars generally experience a disruptive family background, extreme poverty, substance abuse, exclusion from the labour market and often have an acute lack of self-esteem. Many beggars have at some time found themselves victims of harassment from the public. Considerable stigma surrounds people who beg on the streets, and they are often viewed as a threat to society. The beggar has always been an ambiguous figure: an ascetic pilgrim or a lawless wanderer; a deserving object of pity or an undeserving scrounger; a hapless victim of welfare retrenchment or a venal representative of an emergent modern underclass. The beggar is no longer either quaint or pitiable, but is universally reviled (Dean & Melrose, 1999).[29]

There is a much diversity among beggar population. Different types of Beggars could be seen begging around. According to different studies beggars can be categorised as follows:

On the basis of the need, beggars can be classified as *Genuine* and *Fraudulent* – Genuine beggar indicates an individual in dire need who does not misrepresent himself in the course of soliciting donations. Typically, a genuine beggar is unable to engage in alternative economic activities, while a fraudulent beggar is an individual who, while

---

[§]   A 'Vagrant' is homeless migratory non-worker. A 'tramp' is a migratory non-worker. A 'bum' is a stationary non-worker. All these earn their livelihood mainly by begging.

economically downtrodden, intends to misrepresent himself in an effort to gain the benefits that an altruistic donor might be willing to bestow on a genuine beggar. Fraudulent beggar is also poor but he could be engaged in alternative economic activity and purposely chosen begging (Muñoz & Potter, 2013).[30]

On the basis of their physical traits they can be classified as *Old* (elderly) beggars i.e., beggars above the age of 60 years; *Child* beggars i.e. beggars below the age of 14 years; *Disabled* beggars (includes physically handicapped like crippled, blind, deaf etc.); *Able-bodied* beggars i.e., those beggars who are young and seems fit and can be engaged in other work, and; religious *Mendicant* i.e., those beggars who choose begging as prescribed by their religion or sect.[31]

On the basis of reason of begging, beggars can be classified into three categories: beggar by *Circumstances*[32] i.e., those unfortunate individuals who are pushed into begging because of their circumstances like destitution, disruptive family etc.; beggar by *Culture*,[33] there are various communities for whom begging is a hereditary occupation, so they are in begging because of their culture; beggar by *Habit*[34], there are few beggars who even though have family members to support them but still they like to beg as part of their habit (as previously they were in begging). There are some beggars who are so used to begging that they actually prefer not to work.[35]

EXTENT OF BEGGARY: ENUMERATION OF BEGGARS

It is difficult to assess or estimate the population of beggars in any of the city, state or country as a whole. There are number of factors which make it impossible to assess the exact population of beggars. However various studies made attempts to estimate the population of beggars. Hagan and McCarthy (1997)[36] inform us that approximately 100 million children and adolescents live on the streets and are involved in begging worldwide.

Various studies have attempted to estimate the number of beggars in India and in its different cities. In 1945, Kumarappa[37] estimated that there are about 14 lakh beggars in India. In 1957, Moorthy's (1959)[38] study on beggars in Bombay estimated 10,000 beggars in Bombay.

According to M.S. Gore (1959)[39] there were 3,000 beggars in Delhi. In 2004 there were 3,00,000 beggars in Delhi as per Action Aid Report[40]; 75,000 in Kolkata as per Beggar Research Institute[41] and 56,000 in Bangalore according to police records (Malik & Roy, 2012).[42] This data represents the estimation by researchers based on observation and fieldwork.

According to the Government of India Census, 1971, India had a total of 10,11,619 beggars and vagrants, of whom 5,91,501 were male and 4,20,118 females.[43] In the subsequent census surveys, their number decreased considerably. According to Government of India Census, 2001, there were 6,30,940 beggars and vagrants in India in. Out of the total, 3,23,712 (51 per cent) were male and remaining 3,07,228 (49 per cent) were female. West Bengal and Uttar Pradesh were top two states in terms of number of beggars in the same census of the India.

However, as of 2015, as per the official statistics provided by Ministry of Social Justice and Empowerment, Government of India (from census data), there are 4,13,670 beggars and vagrants - 221673 males and 191997 lakh females - in India. West Bengal with 81,244 beggars topped the list followed by 65,835 in Uttar Pradesh, 30,218 in Andhra Pradesh, 29,723 in Bihar and 28,695 in Madhya Pradesh. Incidentally, in Assam, Manipur, and West Bengal female beggars outnumbered their male counterparts. The Union Territories recorded the least number of beggars. The archipelago of Lakshadweep has only two beggars as per the government record, followed by Dadra Nagar Haveli, Daman and Diu and the Andaman and Nicobar Islands with 19, 22 and 56 vagrants respectively. Of all the UTs, Delhi recorded the largest number of vagrants - 2,187 followed by Chandigarh with 121. Among the north-eastern states Assam topped the list with 22,116 beggars while Mizoram with 53 was ranked lowest.[44]

Table 1.1: Total Beggars, Vagrants etc. in India as per Census 2011

S.No.	India/ State/ Union Territory	Beggars, Vagrants etc.		
		Persons	Males	Females
	India	**413670**	**221673**	**191997**
1	Jammu & Kashmir	4134	2550	1584

2	Himachal Pradesh	809	504	305
3	Punjab	7939	5197	2742
4	Chandigarh*	121	87	34
5	Uttarakhand	3320	2374	946
6	Haryana	8682	6504	2178
7	NCT of Delhi*	2187	1343	844
8	Rajasthan	25853	15271	10582
9	Uttar Pradesh	65835	41859	23976
10	Bihar	29723	14842	14881
11	Sikkim	68	46	22
12	Arunachal Pradesh	114	59	55
13	Nagaland	124	65	59
14	Manipur	263	117	146
15	Mizoram	53	33	20
16	Tripura	1490	607	883
17	Meghalaya	396	172	224
18	Assam	22116	7269	14847
19	West Bengal	81244	33086	48158
20	Jharkhand	10819	5522	5297
21	Odisha	17965	9981	7984
22	Chhattisgarh	10198	4995	5203
23	Madhya Pradesh	28695	17506	11189
24	Gujarat	13445	8549	4896
25	Daman & Diu*	22	15	7
26	Dadra & Nagar Haveli*	19	7	12
27	Maharashtra	24307	14020	10287
28	Andhra Pradesh	30218	16264	13954
29	Karnataka	12270	6436	5834
30	Goa	247	131	116
31	Lakshadweep*	2	0	2
32	Kerala	4023	2397	1626
33	Tamil Nadu	6814	3789	3025
34	Puducherry*	99	54	45
35	Andaman & Nicobar	56	22	34

	Islands*			

* Represents a Union Territory of India

Source: Census (2011) Data as provided by Ministry of Social Justice and Empowerment

According to the official data by Census of India 2011, in Jammu and Kashmir there are total 4134 beggars and vagrants, of which 2550 are males and 1584 females. In Jammu City there are 269 individuals (138 males and 131 females) who are identified as beggars and vagrants. However, considering the floating nature of beggar population and their migration patterns, their population keeps changing from time to time.

HISTORICAL BACKGROUND OF BEGGING

In earlier times, until a few centuries ago, begging (and alms-giving) was one of the predominant form of poor relief which was embedded in system of religious belief and duty. In the medieval Europe, as in the Orient, Asia and Middle East, the faithful were exhorted to give alms not only to relieve the poor but also to support travellers and religious pilgrims. Begging practices were cultural resources by which poor and powerless people survived in societies with radical inequalities of wealth and power. Whereas in simple (for example, hunter-gatherer) communities, redistribution was built into the roles and norms through which cooperation among members took place, in peasant economies with military theocratic or feudal socio-political structures, redistribution became a religious duty of the rich and powerful. Begging was one way to remind them of their obligations, when other strategies provided insufficient resources for subsistence (Dean, 1999).[45] Certain forms of begging were morally justified or morally neutral (Jordan, 1999).[46]

There are two prominent views on the origin of beggary and vagrancy. The first view, which may be described as the traditional view, treats beggary and vagrancy as a continuation of the traditional religious practice, with its roots in the religious precepts and social traditions of the past. It highlights the religious motivations and regards all kinds of beggars as persons inspired by an altruistic spirit. Though in modern society and the changed social context the traditional roots of beggary and vagrancy have become less relevant, religion still continues to provide a very strong justification for the phenomenon of beggary, particularly from the point of view of the almsgiver. Perhaps the British government which was interested in the vigorous growth of plantation and industrial capitalism in India in the nineteenth and the twentieth centuries understood this religious nexus. That is why several state committees were appointed to go into the question, mainly to dispel the belief that there is not necessarily any link between religion and beggary. The Bombay Committee observed in this context, "There is a consensus of opinion amongst religious heads of recognized denominations of Hinduism that although begging is permissible among those who renounce the world, the present mode of going a-begging in public streets is unjustifiable" (Pande, 1986).[47]

The second view on the origins of beggary and vagrancy holds that these degrading social conditions are rooted in disorganization, of either the individual or the society. Beggary and vagrancy are perceived in the present context: its roots are located not in past precepts or practices but in the existing individual or social conditions. The first branch-off of this view treats beggary and vagrancy as a product of physical and mental disabilities, personality disorders and defective socialization of the individual: the origin of beggary and vagrancy lies within the individual himself, and thus a beggar is essentially a disorganized person. A variant of the second view relates beggary to the defects in the social and economic structures and the control systems. Explanations of beggary and vagrancy in terms of poverty, calamity and famines, unemployment, landlessness, cultural conflict, the fast rate of social changes, etc. fall within this type of social disorganization. There is yet another and a distinct explanation in the social disorganization theory that is advocated by the Marxist thinkers: beggary and vagrancy are considered a direct offshoot of the capitalist mode of production. This explanation treats beggary and vagrancy not merely as a by-product of capitalism, but also as its inseparable adjunct (Pande, 1986).[48] Karl Marx has described the process of pauperization and criminalization, in the course of the transformation from feudalism to capitalism, thus:

The proletariat created by the breaking-up of the bands of feudal retainers and by forcible expropriation of the people from the soil, this "free" proletariat could not possibly be absorbed by the nascent manufacturers as fast as it was thrown upon the world. On the other hand, these men, suddenly dragged from their wonted mode of life, could not suddenly adapt themselves to the discipline of their new condition. They were turned en masse into beggars, robbers, vagabonds (Marx, 1867).[49]

Subrata Kumar Acharya (1988),[50] is of the view that prior to the Indus Civilization there was no surplus; man lived on the edge of his needs. But in the next, though the North-Western part of India witnessed affluent urban cultures, the rest of this vast country was yet to see the torch of civilization and they solely remained as food-gathering people. Subsequently, when the cultured Aryans came in touch with the constantly migrating nomads, adjustment and maladjustment operated alternatively in the social climate of the then India. The aboriginals to whom agriculture and industry afforded little scope resorted to begging. Later on the rigid *Varnashrama Dharma* of the Brahmins, the austere asceticism of the Jains and the liberal *Shramanic* way of the Buddhists encouraged the homeless life with begging as the sole means of survival. In the centuries immediately preceding and succeeding the Christian era, when most of the religions witnessed split within their folds, the homeless life of the Brahmanas and the *shramanas* corrupted and lost their former significance. To these corrupted *samghas* or ashramas, the poor, destitute, criminals, aboriginals and, above all, persons wounded in battles flocked together for their bare existence. Profession of beggary thus gradually spearheaded and assumed the form of a recognised institution in the so-called Dark age. Though the golden epoch demonstrated an affluent economy, yet in the age of feudalism (c. 500 A.D. - 1200 A.D.) the crisis aggravated alarmingly and the institution of beggary became the evil of evils of the society.

Gillin (1929),[51] argued that if one glances at India one sees other factors at work in producing beggars. From time immemorial tide after tide of migrating peoples has swept into India by land and sea. The great Indian and Mughal empires, which for a few years or centuries gave comparative peace to the land, broke up. Change, however slow, has characterized that land too in the long centuries of its history. Moreover, its religions place a religious value upon the beggar and upon him who contributes. Holy beggars have infested every temple and shrine from time immemorial. Overpopulation, poor resources, and undeveloped industrial methods have reduced the standard of living to a subsistence level even in good times, to starvation in bad.

In India though beggary was there from ancient times, but it was in a much different form than the present one. The present form of begging has emerged mainly due to the introduction of capitalistic form of economy and decline of feudal order of society. The problem of beggary and vagrancy registered a marked growth, and assumed the form of a social menace, only in the 1940s. The emergence of plantation and industrial capitalism in India in the nineteenth and twentieth centuries compelled a large section of the rural population to migrate from rural to urban and industrial centres, mainly as a consequence of the colonial government's policy of planned destruction of the indigenous industrial and trade base. According to the Labour Investigation Committee Report (1943), between the years 1882 and 1943, the working population in factories increased from 3,16,816, to 24,36,312. The number of people who migrated was always much larger than those who gained employment. During the famine years there was in Bengal a mass exodus from the villages to the towns. Ordinarily the presence of a large army of surplus labour was to the advantage of the industrialists who could employ them on their own terms (Pande, 1986).[52] This capitalist logic is explained by the Labour Investigation Committee Report (1943) thus:

There is no doubt that the average worker would prefer even a comparatively low standard of life to the absolute destitution by unemployment.

Thus, in India from earliest known times, begging was prevalent in society. Though in earlier times beggars (mendicants) were seen as ascetic figure who had renounced to worldly pleasures to pursue the religious deeds. In earlier times mostly food and other items of basic needs were given to mendicants or beggars. In only rare occasion they may get money or gold. But, at Present, begging is totally different from previous times as it is not only comprised of the religious mendicants or ascetic person, it is also open for anyone (whether extreme poor, delinquent, lazy or handicapped etc.) who is desirous to do so. In addition, now beggars mostly solicit for money rather than for food or other items of daily need. Some may even refuse if offered food item instead of money.

OBJECTIVES

The study was undertaken with following objectives:

- To explore the sociocultural and economic profile of beggars in Jammu City.
- To study different causes and reasons of begging.
- To study the interactions and encounters of beggars with society (people) and various tools and techniques that beggars use for soliciting alms from people.
- To study various problems faced by beggars in Jammu city.
- To review legal aspect on begging and various governmental provisions and policies (if any) for the welfare/rehabilitation of beggars.

AREA OF THE STUDY

In Jammu and Kashmir, although beggars can be found in almost all cities, towns and some villages too, Jammu City is most preferred place of beggars. This is because most of the beggars in Jammu and Kashmir come from other states of India and Jammu is nearer and bigger than other cities. It also has relatively peaceful environment as compare to some districts/cities of the state (due to militancy). Thus, area chosen for the present study is Jammu city. Jammu is the winter capital (summer capital is Srinagar) of Jammu and Kashmir. It has a population of 503,690 (in 2011 census). In Jammu, beggars are mostly concentrated in the urban areas and in places like - centres for religious worship, railway station, bus/matador stands, commercial and shopping hubs, popular tourist sites, parks, and traffic lights. Jammu is known as the city of temples and has become a popular place of the beggars most of whom come from other parts of the country.

RESEARCH METHODOLOGY

The present study has made use of the Oscar Lewis's theory of the culture of poverty (Lewis, 1959).[53] Lewis's theory of the culture of poverty indicates that poverty as a subculture passes from one generation to another and becomes institutionalized in the poor.

According to Lewis, the lack of effective participation and integration in the major institutions of the larger society is one of the crucial characteristics of culture of poverty. The poor (beggars) feel inferiority complex arising out of the dominant values of society regarding accumulation of status, wealth and property. In their childhood children usually absorb the basic values and attitudes of their sub-culture and are not psychologically geared to take full advantage of changing conditions or increased opportunities which may occur in their lifetime. The theory of culture of poverty indicates that many people are active in begging because of the force of their culture which was internalised in them.

Apart from 'culture of poverty', the concept (theories) of 'Social exclusion' was also taken into consideration to understand begging phenomena. The theorists of social exclusion, stress on its multi-dimensional nature. Social exclusion, they argue, relates not simply to a lack of material resources, but also to matters like inadequate social participation, lack of cultural and educational capital, inadequate access to services and lack of power. In other words, the idea of social exclusion attempts to capture the complexity of 'powerlessness' in modern society rather than simply focusing on one of its outcomes. The term social exclusion has also been most generally used to refer to 'persistent and systematic' multiple deprivation (and processes of disempowerment and alienation), as opposed to poverty or disadvantage experienced for short periods of time (Muddiman, 2000).[54] Though, both 'culture of poverty' (CoP) and 'social exclusion' seems somewhat identical, former (CoP) suggests that it is individuals' fault due to which they remain poor and disadvantaged, while latter asserts that it is system or structure which deprive individuals from basic valuable necessities.

Research Design

Keeping in view the nature of problem under study, both exploratory and descriptive research designs were used. Exploratory design is mainly used where very little may be known about some phenomena such as new types of settings, practices, or groups. While in descriptive design, often, research is initiated to carefully describe a phenomenon or problem in terms of its structure, form, key ingredients, magnitude, and/or changes over time (Pion & Cordray).[55] In context of present study, keeping in view the Beggar population, both designs were suitable and necessary. There was a need to explore the lesser known facts about beggar population and subsequently to describe them.

The study is qualitative as well as quantitative in nature, though, more focus is on qualitative aspect. The data has been collected from both primary and secondary sources. Secondary data was gathered from books, journal articles, periodical articles, reports and a few online web resources. For the primary data, non-participant observation method, Interview and Interview schedule methods are made use of to gather the information. Respondents were observed (by non-participation method) during their begging activity, to understand and interpret their interactions with public and also the techniques they employ to solicit alms. For interaction with respondents, different interview methods were used, like, semi-structured interviews for specific information, in-depth interviews and narrative to get more details on various aspects of their life. Interview schedule (used in semi-structured interviews and in-depth interviews were also based on it) included both close ended as well as open ended questions.

Sampling and sample size

In the Jammu city locations such as religious places, Traffic signals, railway stations, Bus stands, commercial and shopping hubs were selected purposively to interact with the beggars. Some random beggars (who beg in residential areas and inside public vehicles etc.) were also selected.

Table 1.2: Sample Size Details

Area	Male Beggars	Female Beggars	Total
Bus Stand	5	5	10
Traffic Signals	7	3	10
Religious Places	5	5	10
Shopping Hubs/Markets	5	5	10
Random (Other Places)	7	3	10

Total	29	21	50

As the exact size of universe (population of beggars in Jammu) was unknown, the sample has been chosen on the basis of purposive and convenient sampling method. A sample of 50 (10 each from the locations identified above) beggar respondents is selected comprising of both males and females. At few places (can be seen in table) there were less female beggars than their male counterparts, so available female respondents were chosen from those places. To understand the society's views on beggary, 10 random persons (passer-by near begging places) among the general public were briefly interviewed. They were chosen randomly by purposive sampling technique. Views of individuals on various websites and blogs on topic of begging were also taken into consideration. Therefore, the total sample size for the present study was 60, i.e., 50 beggar respondents and 10 non-beggar respondents.

SIGNIFICANCE OF THE STUDY

The present research study is helpful in understanding a disadvantaged and marginalised group i.e. Beggars, their social life, culture, economy and problems. It is also useful in understanding the phenomena of begging in general and particularly in our state. The study helps to have an insight into the life of beggars in Jammu city. Though, one can find literature on beggars of different parts of the country but one hardly finds literature on beggars of Jammu City. Therefore, the study is an addition to the literature on beggars, marginalised groups and will be helpful for both sociologists and policy makers, as it has provided an insight on the problem of beggary.

OUTLINE OF THE BOOK

The Book comprises of five chapter including Introduction and Conclusion. The first chapter **'Introduction'**, includes the statement of the problem, objectives, research methodology, review of literature and significance of the study. It also addresses the historical and social context of contemporary begging. It also discusses the conceptual understanding of begging and also includes a small section dedicated to the field experiences and limitations of the study.

The second chapter **'Socio-cultural and Economic profile of Beggars'**, has looked into the socio-cultural profile of beggars. The primary focus was on the demographic profile (age, sex, religion, education and place of residence etc.) of the respondents, the family and household, the economy (daily earning in begging, savings, scarcity etc.), marriage patterns, and some aspects of their culture. Tables based on primary data, collected during field-work are analysed and discussed in this chapter.

Chapter three, is titled as **'The Beggary Problem: Causes of Begging and State's Response'**. In this chapter both primary and secondary data is used to try to understand "why people beg?" Mostly there are push factors which force people into begging (like destitution, unemployment, disruptive background etc.) and also some pull factors which pull people like (anonymity, no hardwork, freedom of work, etc.). This chapter has also highlighted the discussion on the legal-political aspect of begging in reference to anti-beggary laws and problems faced by beggars.

Chapter four, **'Beggars and Society: Encounters and Techniques,'** focused on interactions that take place between beggars and other members of society. This chapter discussed the stance of society towards begging and beggars, alms giving tradition in various religions and various techniques used by beggars for begging from people.

Chapter five i.e., **'Conclusion'**, is the summary of whole study. It also discussed some of the major conclusions drawn from the study.

FIELD ENCOUNTERS AND LIMITATIONS

The research process involved face-to-face semi-structured interviews with people currently engaged in begging. Begging is a subject which is controversial in itself, as it is an activity which is legally not allowed (illegal) in India as well as in Jammu and Kashmir (though the laws of anti-begging are not implemented properly in most of the places). As Melrose (1999),[56] argued that by choosing to investigate them, the researcher had to enter into "difficult fields of morality, illegality and deviant behaviour" which render both researcher and participants vulnerable. Gaining access to people engaged in begging was not an easy task (as it looks). Firstly, it was very difficult to make them understand about the research as most of them do not know 'what is research?' and even not about the 'University'. Some respondents were very affable and narrated their experiences and stories pleasantly while many were reserved (in terms of talking) and doubtful about the researcher (may be researcher's inquiry about their life) as many repeat this query in response to various sensitive questions, *"Yeh kis liye pooch rahe ho!"* (why are you asking this!), like questions on their parent's occupation, addiction, daily earnings etc. A few beggars refused (some were even rude and aggressive) to be interviewed. Participants were given assurances of confidentiality and were allowed to remain anonymous if they wished. In the event, such assurances seemed irrelevant to many participants because majority of beggars were illiterate and did not understand its relevance.

Gathering the data was a very exposed and public activity as opposed to the (private) intimacy which is often associated with interview situations. It required hanging around the streets, bus stand etc. and conducting interviews on the pavements of the begging sites. Approaching beggars off the begging activity, in their shelters (*Jhuggis* etc.), was considered during initial period of research but later disdained as many denied to be interviewed there and argued that they are not beggars. As author John Healy (1988) who was once himself an alcoholic and vagrant portrays that the world of the beggar is a violent and has frightening environment where those rules of politically correct behaviour that have increasingly come to dominate middle-class lives (especially those of public sector professionals and academics) have completely failed to penetrate (Jordan, 1999).[57]

Some of the narratives of the respondents were so stressful and traumatic that it led to the emotional discomfort of the researcher. However, distancing self from the subjects was learned and adopted during the course of fieldwork to overcome the emotional discomfort. It was a feeling of helplessness (and sometimes guilt) as Researcher was listening to their distressing narratives and then just walk away, unable to offer anything in return which might help them practically. Their motivation for participating in research was mostly a hope that something good will happen to them, although researcher has explained to them that this is just a research (but as discussed earlier they were unfamiliar with research and its purposes). A few participated because they want someone to talk with as usually they do not have people around them for longer conversations.

Some of the limitations in researching beggars and begging activity are listed as:

1. Begging is an illegal activity.
2. The population of beggars is floating in nature. Their settlement place and begging site changes from time to time. Also, they can take break for a few days or few months during which it is difficult to locate them. Complete coverage of areas to enumerate begging is problematic.
3. It is not possible to obtain a representative sample of those who are engaged in begging because of their undefined population.
4. Most of the beggars are illiterate and thus, don't understand about the academic research and its purposes. So, it takes a little effort to illustrate them the meaning of 'Research' and what research is all about.
5. It is difficult to establish a rapport with interviewees (beggars) which is associated with various risks for researchers (interview dynamics). They usually get suspicious while Interview and sometimes does not respond properly.
6. A few beggars prefer anonymous life, though engaged in begging they may never accept that they are beggars.

NOTES

1   Hartley Dean, and Margaret Melrose. 1999. "Easy pickings or hard profession? Begging as an economic activity." In *Begging Questions: Street-level economic activity and social policy failure*, edited by Hartley Dean, 83-100. Bristol: The Policy Press.

2   Madhav Sadashiv Gore. 1958. "Society and the Beggar." *Sociological Bulletin* 7 (1): 23-48. Accessed September 30, 2015. http://www.jstor.org/stable/42864528.

3   David Shichor, and Ruth Ellis. 1981. "Begging in Israel: An exploratory study." *Deviant Behavior* 2 (2): 109-125. doi:10.1080/01639625.1981.9967546.

4   Talcott Parsons. 1951. *The Social System*. London: Routledge & Kegan Paul Ltd.

5   Op. cit. Ref. 4.

6   Hartley Dean, ed. 1999. *Begging Questions: Street-level economic activity and social policy failure*. Bristol: The Policy Press.

7   Op. cit. Ref. 4.

8   Ibid.

9   Op. cit. Ref. 7.

10   J.M. Kumarappa, ed. 1945. *Our Beggar Problem: How to tackle it*. Bombay: Padma Publication Ltd.

11   Tara Patel. 1959. "Some Reflections of the Beggar Problem in Ahmedabad." *Sociological Bulletin* 8 (1): 5-15. Accessed September 30, 2015. http://www.jstor.org/stable/42864545.

12   B.B Pande. 1986. "Rights of Beggars and Vagrants." *India International Centre Quarterly* 13 (4): 115-132. Accessed October 16, 2015. http://www.jstor.org/stable/23001440.

13   Jabir Hasan Khan, Menka, and Shamshad. 2013. "Problems of Beggars: A Case Study." *International Journal of Management and Social Sciences Research (IJMSSR)* 67-74. Accessed March 11, 2016. http://www.irjcjournals.org/ijmssr/Dec2013/11.pdf.

14   Op. cit. Ref. 3.

15   Sanjay Puri. 2015. "Begging in Jammu, a work not compulsion." *State Times*, July 22. Accessed November 4, 2015. http://news.statetimes.in/begging-in-jammu-a-work-not-compulsion/.

16   Op. cit. Ref. 7.

17   Ray Bromley. 1981. "Begging in Cali: Image, Reality and Policy." *International*

Social Work 24 (2): 22-40. doi:10.1177/002087288102400205

18   Op. cit. Ref. 7.

19   Collective for Social Science Research, Karachi. 2004. *A rapid assessment of bonded labour in domestic work and begging in Pakistan.* Working Paper, Geneva: International Labour Office. Accessed October 4, 2015.

20   Op. cit. Ref. 7.

21   Eugene Bardach, and Eric M. Patashnik. 2006. *A Practical Guide for Policy Analysis: The Eightfold Path to More Effective Problem Solving.* 5th. Washington DC: CQ Press.

22   Oscar Lewis. 1998. "The Culture of Poverty." *Society* 35 (2): 7-30. doi:10.1007/BF02838122.

23   Op. cit. Ref. 16.

24   Christopher R. Stones. 2013. "A psycho-social exploration of street begging: A qualitative study." *South African Journal of Psychology* 43 (2): 157-166. doi:10.1177/0081246313482632.

25   Sandra Frink. 2010. "Strangers are Flocking Here: Identity and Anonymity in New Orleans, 1810-1860." *American Nineteenth Century History* 11 (2): 155-181. doi:10.1080/14664658.2010.481869.

26   Op. cit. Ref. 12.

27   Michael Horn, and Michelle Cooke. 2011. *A Question Of Begging: A study of the extent and nature of begging in the City of Melbourne.* Research Study, Melbourne: Hanover.

28   2016. *Begging for Life- From Manila to Malmo (Documentary).* Directed by Barnaby Phillips and Karim Shah. Performed by Al Jazeera English. Accessed August 23, 2016. http://www.aljazeera.com/programmes/peopleandpower/2016/01/begging-life-160126130424263.html.

29   Op. cit. Ref. 2.

30   Cristian Pérez Muñoz, and Joshua D Potter. 2013. "Street-level charity: Beggars, donors, and welfare policies." *Journal of Theoretical Politics* 26 (1): 158-174. doi:10.1177/0951629813493836.

31   Op. cit. Ref. 11.

32   Op. cit. Ref. 7.

33 Op. cit. Ref. 23.

34 Op. cit. Ref. 12.

35 S. Cook, "India Beggars and Begging Scams: What You Should Know." *About Travel (about.com)*. Accessed July 2, 2016.
http://goindia.about.com/od/annoyancesinconveniences/p/indiabegging.htm.

36 John Hagan, and Bill McCarthy. 1998. *Mean Streets: Youth Crime and Homelessness.* Cambridge: Cambridge University Press. 1998

37 Op. cit. Ref. 11,

38 M.Vasudeva Moorthy. 1959. *Beggar Problem in Greater Bombay: A Research Study.* A Research Study, Bombay: Indian Conference of Social Work.

39 M.S. Gore, J.S. Mathur, M.R. Laljani, and H.S Takulia. 1959. *The Beggar Problem in Metropolitan Delhi.* Delhi: School of Social Work

40 Sonia Malik, and Sanjoy Roy. 2012. "A Study on Begging: A Social Stigma-An Indian Perspective." *Journal of Human Values* 18 (2): 187-199. doi:10.1177/0971685812454486.

41 Ibid.

42 Ibid.

43 Op. cit. Ref. 13.

44 PTI. 2015. "Over 4 lakh beggars in India, most in West Bengal: Govt." *The Indian Express*, August 13. Accessed January 15, 2016.
http://indianexpress.com/article/india/india-others/over-4-lakh-beggars-in-india-most-in-west-bengal-govt/

45 Op. cit. Ref. 7.

46 Bill Jordan. 1999. "Begging: the global context and international comparisons." In *Begging Questions: Street-level economic activity and social policy failure*, edited by Hartley Dean, 43-62. Bristol: The policy Press.

47 Op cit. Ref. 13.

48 Ibid.

49 Karl Marx. 1867. *Capital: A Critique of Political Economy.* Edited by Frederick Engels. Translated by Samuel Moore and Edward Aveling. Vol. I. Moscow: Progress Publishers. Accessed October 21, 2015.
https://www.marxists.org/archive/marx/works/1867-c1/.

[50] Subrata Kumar Acharya. 1988. "Evolution of The Institution of Beggary in Ancient India." *Annals of the Bhandarkar Oriental Research Institute* 69 (1): 269-277. Accessed September 30, 2015. http://www.jstor.org/stable/41693775

[51] J. L. Gillin. 1929. "Vagrancy and Begging." *American Journal of Sociology* 35 (3): 424-432. Accessed May 21, 2016. http://www.jstor.org/stable/2765752.

[52] Op cit. Ref. 13.

[53] Oscar Lewis. 1959. *Five Families: Mexican Case Studies in the Culture of Poverty*. New York: Basic Books.

[54] Dave Muddiman. 2000. "Theories of social exclusion and the public library." In *Open to All? : the Public Library and Social Exclusion*, by Dave Muddiman, 1-15. London: The Council for Museums, Archives and Libraries.

[55] Georgine M. Pion, and David S. Cordray. n.d. "Research Methods." *Encyclopedia of Education*. Accessed December 18, 2015. http://www.encyclopedia.com.

[56] Margaret Melrose. 1999. "Word From the Street: Perils and Pains of Researching Begging." In *Begging Questions: Street-level Economic Activity and Social Policy Failure*, by Hartley Dean, 143-161. Bristol: The Policy Press.

[57] Op. cit. Ref. 47.

2: SOCIOCULTURAL AND ECONOMIC PROFILE OF BEGGARS

A sociocultural profile is a description of a group (sample) or research setting. It is description about their society and culture which includes demography, religion, various institutions (like Family Marriage etc.), their economic activities and so on. In research, it is used to understand the context (situation) of a particular social problem. This chapter has, therefore, tried to look into the socio-cultural and economic life of the beggars in Jammu city.

The beggar population in Jammu is not a homogeneous one. It includes people from different religions, caste, ethnicity, regions, and cultures. The only parameter which categorise them as one group is their economic activity i.e., begging. However, according to Marx's economic determinism we can find various similarities among these different groups or individuals due to their same economic activity and economic conditions. There are some local beggars which are from different parts of Jammu and Kashmir like Rajouri, Udhampur, Akhnoor, Samba, Anantnag etc. The others are from various states of the India - mostly from Chhattisgarh, Rajasthan, Uttar Pradesh, Madhya Pradesh, Maharashtra, Haryana, Punjab, Bihar etc.

In present research study, during the fieldwork, it was observed that there were very less local (from J&K) 'able-bodied young persons' engaged in begging. Local beggars who were engaged in begging were mostly disabled, old and weak, widows and persons who were abandoned by their family. Mostly they beg by sitting in some fixed place like Bus Stand and practice much of a passive type of begging (they don't run after or irritate a passer-by). Most of them don't beg throughout the year. They beg for some months and when they get enough money they take rest for next few months (usually return to their homes, if they have one) and return back when they run short of money. One disabled from Mansar, J&K who beg in bus stand narrates his story as briefed and translated below.

"I was disabled (his both legs were paralysed) by birth. My parents didn't like me much because of my disability. My siblings and cousins bullied me and made fun of my disability. I could not understand what to do about my situation… After my younger brother's marriage my family forced me leave home as they felt ashamed of me in front of their new relatives. My health was deteriorated and I become weak… With the help of a neighbour I came to Jammu for treatment in GMC. I was sitting outside the hospital, a stranger came and gave me a coin then some more followed. That was the moment I realised that this is the way for me to earn my livelihood and I started begging from people… After one year I went back to my home and with the help of police I got my share of parental property – a few Kanals of land and a Kachha house. Now I regularly go back to my village after few months of begging in Jammu and stay there especially during hot summer. A neighbour friend of mine takes care of my property and land during my absence. He cultivates my piece of land and gives half of the produce from it to me… But I have to earn money to buy other necessary items like Oil, clothes, soap etc. for which I am still engaged in seasonal begging… In Jammu I don't have any shelter to live and I sleep near Police Chowki (Bus Stand) for security from thieves. I earn around `200 daily but spent `50-100 daily on food and other necessary items. Though I still feel bad about my life, but when I remember the earlier days I feel a bit relieved."

Non-local beggars comprise of all type of beggars – able bodied young persons, religious beggars, and all. Some of the non-local (migrant) beggars live as group ('*Dera*') and assert that begging is their traditional hereditary occupation. Most of the able bodied beggars are from these type of *Deras*. While begging, they (occupational beggar) may use snakes, appeal cards or some instruments. They wear a traditional dress representing themselves as religious persons but different from sadhus. A woman (begging outside Shalimar Hospital) dressed in saffron and carrying a snake said: "*Almost all persons of our dera practise begging. It is our hereditary occupation… We worship 'Nag devta' (referring to snake that she was carrying with her) and keep it with us while begging.*"

There are many others individual migrant beggars. These individual beggars live with their families or alone in their *jhuggis* or also live in clusters with other beggars (who are either their friends or from same state as they are) or labourers and other casual workers of their native states. They have migrated because of the fact that begging is a stigmatised and shameful activity and they could not beg in their native villages/towns. Moreover, some of them argued that Jammu city is full of generous people which is the basic need of begging "profession". While most of the beggars have normal family life (family either with them in Jammu or in their native villages), some do have very disruptive family backgrounds. A story as narrated by a female beggar who begs in *Rehari* area is briefed as below:

"*I don't know about my parents or my birth place… I was raised up by a man in slums perhaps in Delhi or near* (as she did not recall or don't have the exact knowledge about that place) … *When I was still a child* (about 6-7 years old) *he sold me to another man (in marriage) who was much older* (about 30 years older than her) *than me and had problem of mental illness… His mother used me for begging… Initially she used to beat me when I refused to go for begging as at that time I really hated begging… I had no other place to live so I had to obey her and did whatever she wanted from me… Now I have two children* (one she was carrying with her while begging) *and now I have compromised and adapted to my situation… I have to beg for rest of my life as it has now become a routine (habit) for me… I beg for 4-5 days a week and on other days of week I take rest and do other household work at home* (a kachha house in Muthi Gaon)… *I usually make around ` 150 daily… I am not able to save money and many times I am left with no money…*"

DEMOGRAPHIC PROFILE OF THE RESPONDENTS

Demography is concerned with how large (or small) populations are – that is, their size; how the populations are composed according to age, sex, race, marital status, and other characteristics – that is, their composition; and how populations are distributed in physical space, for example how urban and rural they are – that is, their spatial distribution. Of equal or greater importance, demography is interested in the changes over time in the size, composition, and distribution of populations, as these result from the processes of fertility, mortality, and migration (B. S. Turner 2006)[58]. In present study some these demographic factors of beggar respondents are explored which are discussed as follows.

Age

Age is a parameter through which we can locate the stages of life of individuals. There are age sets (stages) that define the social status, roles and patterns of behaviour appropriate for those who belong to them. In many simple societies, age sets are a crucial element of the social structure, but even in industrial societies age remains an important variable for the allocation of legal rights and responsibilities. The chronological process of growing older obviously has a biological basis: the human physique and its associated capacities change over time in a manner that is regular, even if the timing of changes varies from person to person. Sociological interest in ageing concentrates on the social expectations that we have of the elderly. At its simplest, there is a clear contrast between the way that many traditional societies regard their oldest members (as repositories of wisdom and experience) and the relatively low status that modern societies offer the elderly (Bruce and Yearley 2006)[59].

The study of age in sociology includes, influences affecting individuals across all phases of the life course, as well as the specific period known as old age. Social policy and government interests in old age because they often view old age as a problem (for the economy or the health service, to take two examples). (B. S. Turner 2006)[60]

Most participants (in present study) were vague about their exact ages and said that they did not remember due to lack of any documents, several said that either they had lost their ID proof or that it had been stolen and some said they never had one. However, they provided a rough estimation of their age which was recorded by researcher considering their physical traits.

Table 2.1: Age of the Respondents

Age	No. of Respondents	Males	Females	Percentage
18-30	6	2	4	12
31-50	17	8	9	34
51-70	18	11	7	36
71 and above	9	8	1	18
Total	**50**	**29**	**21**	**100**

The data in the above table shows that most of the beggars are in the age group of 51-70 years (36%) followed by 31-50 years (34%), 71 and above (18%) and age group of 18-30 years (12%). Thus, most of the beggars were above 30 years of age, excluding child beggars which were not included in the study. While most males are concentrated between age group of 51-70, and most females are in age group of 31-50 years.

From this data on age of beggars in Jammu, it is evident that usually they start begging at a later stage of life mostly when they face prolonged poverty and unemployment. Some beggars started begging at later stage of life because they were physically unable to do any other work and had no one to support them financially. *"Jab tak zor tha to mazdori krta tha ab kamzori ki wajah se koi aur kaam ni kr skta."* [(I) was a labourer till there was strength in my body now due to weakness I could not do any other work].

Religion

Religion is a system (institution) of belief and practices. A sense of obligation usually attaches to these beliefs and practices, and they confer a sense of collective identity on believers. In begging context religion plays a fundamental role by encourage almsgivings (donations) to poor. Every religion in the world as well as in India encourages helping the poor and needy by donating whatever one could. However, it also prescribes precautions while selecting the poor and needy; and circumstances/conditions when an individual can solicit for alms.

Table 2.2: Religion of the Respondents

Religion	No. of Respondents	Percentage
Hindu	32	64
Muslim	15	30
Sikh	2	4
No Religion	1	2
Total	**50**	**100**

The religion of beggar respondents in Jammu shows that there are more Hindu (64%) beggars in Jammu but also a significant number of Muslim beggars (30%). Sikhs were 4% (i.e. 2) of total respondents while one beggar responded that he believes in no God (or all Gods, 'it does not matter'). It can be noted that Jammu is known as a city of temples and have majority population of Hindus which can be the reason of more Hindu beggars here. It was also observed that beggars preferred begging in religious places associated with their own religion but there was no strict restriction. Few Muslim beggars were found in Hindu religious places and vice-versa.

Marx notion of religion as the 'opium of masses'[61] holds ground in beggar population as they strongly believed that its God's will and (or) their karma in previous life (or in this life) that made them beggars. *"Bhagwan ki marzi ke khilaf kya ho sakta hai, kiye honge kuch aise karm pichle janam mein"* [Nothing could happen without God's will, may be its due to my Karma in previous life].

Education

Education is backbone of modern society. Educational sociology focused on the contribution of education to social mobility and life-chances, social class differences in educational attainment and the explanation of these (Abercrombie, Hill and Turner 1984)[62].

In a study on beggars in Delhi, Malik and Roy (2012),[63] observed that most of the beggars were less educated, with 60 per cent of them who had never been to school and 26 per cent of them left the school at a very young age, which is again a very high percentage. To make matters worse, they all join this profession before they reach 8th standard. Only

14 per cent of the beggars sent their wards to the schools.

In Tara Patel's (1959)[64] study out of 100 beggars 63 were illiterate and 37 literates. In a few cases the standard of literacy was high; one was graduate, one matriculate and five had studied upto high school standard. The number of literate females is much smaller. This is another factor limiting the scope of the rehabilitation programme of the beggars.

Table 2.3: Education of the Respondents

Education Qualification	No. of Respondents	Percentage
Illiterate	43	86
Up to 5th	4	8
5th – 10th	3	6
Above 10th	Nil	0
Total	**50**	**100**

As shown in table above 43 (86%) of total beggar respondents were illiterate (no formal education), four (8%) were educated up to primary, and three (6%) were educated up to secondary level, while no beggar respondent was educated more than secondary (10th) level. Thus, most of the beggar population (in the present study) were illiterate. Lack of education (coupled with ignorance) was prominent among them due to which they remained unemployable and unmotivated for any progress or mobility (economic and cultural) that life could offer them. Due to illiteracy they also lacked skills that are needed for employment in modern world where unskilled (and uneducated) persons are unfit for any work except manual labour. However, in the study, it was also found that there was some awareness about the role of education among beggars and some of them send (or want to send) their children to school.

Native States of the Beggars (From where these people come?)

Begging is an activity associated with anonymity, shame and social exclusion.

Table 2.4: Native states of Beggar the respondents

State	No. of Respondents	Percentage
Jammu and Kashmir	6	12
Rajasthan	7	14
Chhatisgarh	7	14
UP	6	12
MP	5	10
Maharashtra	2	4
Bihar	4	8
Haryana	2	4
Punjab	2	4
Jharkhand	2	4
No Response	7	14
Total	**50**	**100**

So to avoid shame, most of the beggars preferred working/begging away from their homes. As stated earlier, during fieldwork very less number of local beggars were found in begging in Jammu city. Majority of the beggars came from other nearby states.

It is clearly evident from above table that most of the beggars in Jammu and Kashmir were from other states of India. Among the beggar respondents only six (12%) were local beggars i.e., from J&K. Other states from where these beggars migrate to Jammu were Chhattisgarh (14%), Rajasthan (14%), Uttar Pradesh (12%), Madhya Pradesh (10%), Bihar (8%), Maharashtra (4%), Punjab (4%), Haryana (4%) and Jharkhand (4%). While five beggars (14%) didn't reply (or didn't know exactly as they were sold or deserted at an early age) satisfactorily to this question. Some migrant beggars responded that they are in J&K from last almost 30 to 50 years (Like Kanpuria in Rajiv Nagar Narwal and other Deras) and permanently left their native states as they had no land there, while many others said that they were in this city from roughly around last 1 to 10 years.

Begging is a shame if one has social relations with rest of the society, so when they had to beg they usually migrate to new places where no one could recognise them. *"Ghar ke paas mangne mein thoda sharam rehta hai"* [Begging near hometown is little awkward and shameful]. In begging occupation (or begging circles or profession) beggars have to compete with fellow beggars to earn more so they migrate to different places where they could earn good amount and where they could feel safer and stable. And when they get these parameters in any place, they settle there for relatively long time. Jammu seems to have this attraction and is becoming a destination of beggars.

Shichor and Ellis (1981)[65] also observed in their study that all the beggars interviewed were working outside of their own neighbourhoods; half of them came to the city from satellite towns, sometimes traveling long distances. The usual reasons being given for this were that they were embarrassed to beg in their own neighbourhoods and that the big city afforded more lucrative business.

Present Residence

In Jammu beggars are spreaded all over the city. Some have established relatively permanent settlements, others have temporary. During the study, it was found that beggars were living in *Jhuggis* or *Kachha* houses mainly in the areas like- Belicharana, Rani Bagh, Vijaypur, Marathi Mohalla Trikuta Nagar, Raje Chak Akhnoor, Bage-e-Bahu, Raghunath Market, Railway Station, Bohri Talab Tillo, Kanpuria Basti Rajiv Nagar Narwal, Empty Space under Fly Over, Bus Stand JDA complex, Panjtirthi, Muthi Gaon National Highway Nagrota, Thandi Khui, Mishriwala etc.

Though some beggars managed accommodation (shelter – *jhuggi* or rough sleeping) nearby their area of begging, others have shelter away (about distance of 5-15km) from their favourite begging sites. Every day they travel by local matadors from their places (shelters) to begging sites and back home.

Migration/Rotation Patterns

There is a positive relation between begging and migration. Migration and rotation is the core element of begging. Though some beggars beg at some fixed places, majority of beggars are in a continuous cycle of migration and rotation.

Patel (1959)[66] in a study on beggars in Ahemadabad found that out of the 100 beggars only 18 were local residents and 72 migrated from other parts of the country. When they were questioned about the causes of their migration to the city they reported:

i) Poverty due to various reasons such as debt, loss of crop, etc. in search of job, for earning *ii*) For the sake of begging *iii*) Migrated with parents or other relatives *iv*) Loss of interest in the family and in the world; family quarrels; family calamity such as loss of husbands, parents, etc. *v*) Migratory habits *vi*) Not known

Table 2.5: Migration/Rotation Patterns of the Respondents

Migration/Rotation Patterns	No. of Respondents	Percentage
No Migration/Rotation	15	30
On Rotation in Jammu	23	46
Migrate to other Places	12	24
Total	**50**	**100**

As evident from above data, beggar usually practiced a rotation policy. Though some beggars sit at one particular place (30%) for begging, most of them beg at different places on the different days of the week, i.e., they follow rotation technique (46%). Some beggars also migrate (24%) to other places, especially to Kashmir region due to hot summer in Jammu. As most of the beggars in Jammu city are migrated from other states of India they can migrate to other states when they face some serious problems here. A beggar narrated his rotation scheme in Jammu City:

"On Monday I beg at Shankar Mandir Trikuta Nagar; on Tuesday and Sunday at Bawe (outside the Kali Mata Mandir); on Wednesday at Bikram Chowk and Raghunath Market; on Thursday at Gandhi Nagar area; on Friday again in Trikuta Nagar area; and on Saturday at Railway Station Jammu. I prefer religious places for begging."

Therefore, it can be said that rotation technique was used by them to earn more and they also had identified the areas (for begging) over a period of time which could help them to earn more.

FAMILY AND HOUSEHOLD

Family is basic and most important institution in human society. It socialises individuals and plays an important role in shaping his personality. In short, individual is what family makes him. Since family is primary and a very powerful agent of social approbation, it may be regarded as the most important of the social ties. While discussing socio-cultural life of beggars it is necessary to have a look on their family structure. The Census of India, defined 'household' as "a group of persons who normally live together and take their meals from a common kitchen unless the exigencies of work prevent any of them from doing so. Persons in a household may be related or unrelated or a mix of both. However, if a group of unrelated persons live in a census house but do not take their meals from the common kitchen, then they are not constituent of a common household. Each such person was to be treated as a separate household".[67]

Gore (1958)[68] in his study found that out of the 600 beggars, 25% had no families either parental or their own. Of the rest, 20% lived with their families. These families were either parental, conjugal or joint. Out of the remaining about 5% gave no information, and 50% lived away from their families. The actual number of those living away from their families - because the families became extinct or because they had voluntarily moved out of them is, thus, found to be (50+25=75%) of the total number of beggars. Gore further argued that the fact that a person is living away from his family is no indication that he is isolated from it. He may still be in touch with the family. He, therefore, sought to find out the nature of contact, if any, he had with his family. In his study, he found that only 10% or the beggars stayed away from their families and still had a regular contact with them. The others had either a very perfunctory or no contact at all with their families. Thus while 50% of the beggars had their families and lived away from them, there were at least 40% who had no contact with them. It may be said that a person who is isolated from his family is not necessarily a social isolate. A beggar may have broken with his home and yet he may have other social relationships and companions either within the group of beggars or outside it.

Type of Family (Before and After)
Table 2.6: Family type of the Respondents

Family Type	Before Begging	Percent age	At Present	Percent age
No family	6	12	15	30
Nuclear	13	26	28	56
Joint	29	58	6	12
No Response	2	4	1	2
Total	**50**	**100**	**50**	**100**

Before coming into begging activity 29 (58%) beggars have had a joint family, while 13 (26%) beggars were from nuclear family, 6 (12%) beggars had no family and 2 (4%) beggars didn't respond satisfactorily. However, at present, after coming into begging activity, this scenario has completely changed. Now Number of beggars having joint family has reduced to 6 (12%) only. However, now 28 (56%) beggar live in nuclear family, while 15 (30%) are living alone without any family and one (2%) beggar didn't respond about present type of family.

Before coming into begging, as most of the respondents were dependents on other family members, so they were staying with them in a joint family. But after starting begging when they started earning, they separated from their joint family as they were no longer dependent on other members of their family. Therefore, the data clearly indicates that begging has led to nuclearisation of families.

Shelter Type – Facilities, Problems and condition
Table 2.7: Type of Shelter/House of the Respondents

Shelter Type	No of Respondents	Percentage
Jhuggi	24	48
Kaccha House	6	12
Pacca House	3	6
Room on Rent	4	8
No Shelter	13	26
Total	**50**	**100**

Shelter is one of the fundamental need of humans. Generally significant numbers of beggars do not have shelter and those who have shelter are living in very poor houses (Namwata and Mgabo 2012).[69] It was found that most of the beggars (48%) in Jammu City live in *Jhuggis* (Slums). Those beggars who resided in *jhuggis* were the migrants from others states and were living with other people (they can be beggars or migrant labourers) from their native states. It provided them a sense of security and support. Each family had their own *jhuggi* and those didn't have their families with them or had no family, were either living alone or were sharing the *jhuggi* with other persons of similar profile…. Some beggars lived in *Rented Rooms* (12%). In this category are both local as well migrant beggars. It is because they managed to find the affordable (low rent) rooms and due to the support of the landlord (house owners). They either earned comparatively more than others or had some other family member to contribute. Some other beggars had *Kaccha House* (8%) to live. They were either local beggars or migrants who were begging in Jammu for relatively longer period and usually don't migrate to other places. There were also many beggars who had *No Shelter* (26%) and usually sleep in open (rough-sleep). They were either temporary migrant beggars who are in Jammu for a short period or local beggars who came from outside of Jammu city (like Rajouri, Udhampur) and beg for a short period and then return back to their homes. A few beggars also reported to have *Pacca Houses* (6%) where they lived with other family members. They were widows or other elderly persons who were the sole breadwinners of their family and had no other family member for financial support. However, they visited their homes daily and slept near their working location.

How Family members treat the beggar

When other family members of a beggar are not engaged in begging and can earn through other works like labour and other better options, they try to stop them from begging. *"Family members try to stop me from begging but I have to earn so that I can take care of myself in better way"*.

While most of the beggars responded that they were treated normally, with love by family members. In many such cases, other family members were also engaged in begging or other related activity like rag-picking etc. as they had no other source of income. Due to extreme conditions (poverty and unemployment) which beggars as well as their family members were facing (have faced) they feel begging normal as it provided them a livelihood.

A few responded that that their family members hated and avoided and them even before coming into begging due to their disability and also because they are incapable to do any work to earn a livelihood. Here hate by family members can be cause or factor responsible for the begging.

Authority Structure

Table 2.8: Head of the Family

Head	No. of Respondents	Percentage
Male Head	20	40
Female Head	15	30
No Family	15	30
Total	**50**	**100**

Authority structure (or power relations) in a family give various information related to gender discourse. Among Beggars respondents, in present study (total 50), 20 (40%) beggars said that they had male heads in their family, 15 (30%) said that they were from female headed household and 15 (30%) said that they had no family (so question of head of the family does not apply to them). The female headed households were the ones where women were widows and were therefore the sole earner (as beggar) in the family and thus, become the head of the household.

Dependents

Table 2.9: Number of dependents

Dependents	No. of Respondents	Percentage
No Dependent	20	40
1-2	18	36

3-5	10	20
6 and above	2	4
Total	**50**	**100**

On question of the number of dependents, 20 (40%) beggars said that they earn for themselves as they have no family or other family members also engaged in same or some other activity. 18 (36%) beggars said that they have 1 or 2 family members who directly dependent on them. 10 (20%) beggars said that they have 3-5 dependents while only two (4%) respondents said that they have six or more dependents. During the study it was observed that the dependents were mainly children. The issue of the size of family (number of children) or more dependents, did not bothered them as they believed that more numbers (of children) means more hands to earn.

Views Towards Education of Children

Table 2.10: Children's Education of respondents

Send Children to Schools	No. of Respondents	Percentage
Yes	14	28
No	20	40
Not Applicable	16	32
Total	**50**	**100**

Although most beggars in present study were illiterate but some of them want their children to get education. Some of them were optimistic about the role of education, as an institution, to bring change in their condition. Fourteen (28%) beggar respondents send their children to schools, while 20 (40%) beggars don't send their children to the school as they believe earning is more important than education and they strongly believed in begging as an easy mode to earn. This also depicts that it is because of culture of poverty that they don't want to come out of their situation. Sixteen (32%) beggars don't have children.

MARRIAGE PATTERNS

Marriage along with family is also a basic institution of human society. Its primary aim is to regulate sex relation in a society and provide a stable order for procreation. Like every individual in a society, marriage (as an institution) also holds a prominent position among beggars. It is both individually desirable as well as a social need.

Marital Status

Table 2.11: Marital Status of the Respondents

Marital Status	No. of Respondents	Males	Females	Percentage
Unmarried	11	9	2	22
Married	18	13	5	36
Widowed	19	7	12	38
Divorced	1	0	3	4
Total	**50**	**29**	**21**	**100**

On Inquiring about the question of marital status of the beggars, it was found that there was not any significant difference in number of beggars on the basis of marital status as 19 (38%) beggars were widow/widower, followed by Married (36%), Unmarried (22%) and Divorced (4%). However, when one observes the marital status on the basis of gender, most of the men beggar respondents were married while women respondents in begging were mostly widows. It can, therefore, be concluded that livelihood is the only force for which people have to beg. In Indian society, married men are responsible for earning bread for their family and when there is no male head in family, the female head (usually widow or divorced) is responsible for the same. So marital status and in turn the authority and responsibility which they gain through it is a prime force for begging activity.

It was also found that the male beggars get married at an average age of about 20 years and female beggars at about 14 years. Beggars are from poor and traditional type of family background where members get married at early age especially females (generally after reaching puberty stage).

Mate Selection and Partner Preference

As beggars do not constitute a single community, they follow different norms of their respective societies while mate selection. Most beggars agreed that generally marriage partner is selected with consent of the parents of couple (to be married). However, even if couple get married without their parents' permission it is not a stigma for them. One finds the patrilocal residence among the beggars also.

Role of caste/class in Marriage

Beggars also follow caste system and marry within their caste or equivalent group. In India within the caste also, one finds that there is class consideration while selecting partner for marriage. Among the beggars of Jammu one finds that they prefer marrying in a beggar community (and in his/her own caste) though some of them married outside this group with other groups of almost similar social status (like rag pickers etc.).

Dowry

On being asked about the practice of dowry, almost all beggars agreed to have this custom and generally responded in this phrase *"who to zaruri hai"* (that is must). It is given as per bride's parents' choice. Two beggar respondents said that they give dowry items of approximately ` 1,00,000. While most of the respondents said that usually they give these items in dowry like- TV, Cooler, Beddings, Utensils etc. Most of them agreed to have given/taken the dowry, but restrained from giving exact (detailed) information about it.

CULTURE – FESTIVALS, FOOD PATTERNS

Namwata and Mgabo (2012)[70] observed that street beggars do not have neat or sufficient clothes to suit changing weather conditions and are usually bare footed. Most of them use one and same clothes during the days and nights. Interview with street beggars indicated that street beggars mostly assume that if they wear better clothes they wouldn't be successful while begging for alms. Same scenario was observed during the present study too, as many beggars were seen in dirty and torn clothes in begging sites and on the pavements.

Festivals

Beggar respondents admitted that they celebrate all major festivals as per their religion, caste and region. Like Hindu Beggars celebrates festivals like Holi, Diwali, Lori etc. Muslims observe Ramadan and Eid.

Rituals and Celebrations

Each beggar or group of beggars practice different rituals. There are three basic ceremonies which are observed in every society – Birth, Marriage and Death. Beggars also have different rituals with regard to these basic ceremonies. All the beggars said that Birth and Marriages are ceremonies of happiness and joy and they celebrate these by inviting their near and dears and offering them meal, *Daaru* (alcohol) etc. They use musical instruments like *Dhol* (drums), and sing songs for entertainment. During the interaction, it was found that though, son preference was there among many beggars but even the birth of a daughter was also celebrated as for them, it was the new earning member added to their family.

Food Patterns

Namwata and Mgabo (2012)[71] observed that beggars normally obtain their daily meal requirements and that of their family from different sources. It was reported that most of the street beggars got their daily meals as leftover food (makombo) from hotels, restaurants, markets, garbage bins, dump sites and individual residential areas. These seem to be major sources of daily meals for street beggar's themselves and their families or people staying with them. Sometimes street beggars get *makombo* (Tanzanian term for leftover food) from hotels or restaurants or individual residential areas in exchange of emptying garbage, carrying loads, gardening, cleaning and washing dishes. Other street beggars bought their own food using their income or small amount of money collected in a day. They buy foods usually from small tea houses, street cafe's and food vendors. The last source of meals for street beggars is from good Samaritans, NGOs, church yards, individual residences and other business community though not common.

Table 2.12: Number of Meals

Meals/Day	No. of Respondents	Percentage
1	Nil	0
2	30	60
3	20	40
Total	**50**	**100**

As observed during the fieldwork, many beggars were malnutritioned, it was asked from the beggar respondents that how many meals they have in a day. Thirty (60%) beggars said that they take only two meals daily while Twenty (40%) beggars take three meals daily. In Jammu, beggars mostly get at least one meal as alms from others. The free meal could be given by some individuals or leftovers from *dhaba* (small roadside food points) or *langer/bhandara* (a kind of feast) in temple. However, many beggars (especially who have families with them) prepare at least one meal at home. Individual (single/alone) beggars argued that sometime during the day when they do not get any meal as alms, they buy it for themselves from *Dhabas*.

"Sham ko ghar mein mein hi bnate hain… Din ko mandir mein bhandara hota hai to wahan kha lete hain ya Prasad (halwa puri) mil jata hai kabhi, aur kabhi na mile to dhabe pe kha lete hain piase de ke." [(I) prepare my dinner at home only…During day (I) usually get meal from temple if there is a *Bhandara* (feast) or as *prasad* and when (i) don't get meal from temple I buy it from *Dhaba*].

Table 2.13: Food Preference

Preference	No. of respondents	Percentage
Vegetarian	28	56
Non-Vegetarian	22	44
Total	**50**	**100**

Among total 50 respondents, 28 (56%) beggars said that they were vegetarian while 22 (44%) acknowledged that though they mostly take vegetarian food, sometime they also take non-vegetarian food (mostly chicken or eggs).

Addiction

Tara Patel (1959)[72] observed that the beggars are not without wasteful expenses. Many of them were found in the habit of taking tea. A few of them smoked and a smaller number of them was found addicted to *Ganja* (a drug), a prohibited article. Many of these beggars spent whatever they earned on tea, pan bidi and occasionally on cinema. The average daily amount spent on such items by a beggar in our enquiry was approximately ` 5-10 (in 1959).

Table 2.14: Addiction among respondents

Addiction	No of Beggars	Percentage
No Addiction	5	10
Tobbaco Products only	9	18
Tobacco+Alcohol	31	62
No Response	5	10
Total	**50**	**100**

Addiction was common among beggars. Only five (10%) beggars said that they were not addicted to any tobacco product or alcohol. Nine (18%) beggars said that they only take tobacco product (like *Beedi, Kheni* etc.), a majority i.e., thirty-one (62%) beggars said that they were addicted to both Tobacco products and Alcohol (mostly desi whisky pouch commonly known as '*Frooti*'). Tobacco is used as daily addiction while alcohol consumption varies from beggar to beggar. Some may consume it on daily basis and others occasionally. However, from these figures one cannot draw the conclusion that beggars are mostly alcoholic and beg to support their addiction. If we look at alcohol consumption pattern of other people in Jammu city[**] we may find these figure normal as alcohol consumption is becoming a cultural habit among poor,

---

[**] According to J&K government 556.67 lakh bottles of liquor including Indian manufactured foreign liquor (IMFL), Desi Whiskey, beer and ready to drink liquor were sold in 2015 as compared to 546.51 lakh bottles in 2014 thereby registering an increase of 10.16 lakh bottles.

middle class and equally among rich.[73]

ECONOMY

Begging is an economic activity or to be brief, a livelihood. People engage themselves in begging to earn money to fulfil their needs for survival.

Personal income of 46 per cent beggars is greater than 1,500 per month and 14 per cent of them are just below the poverty line by earning around ` 500 per month. Most of them work (40.5 per cent) for 6 to 9 hours a day and only 21 per cent of them work for more than 9 hours a day. (Malik and Roy 2012)[74]

Namwata and Mgabo (2012),[75] argued regarding the amount of money collected in a good day. They said that a large population of street beggars (31.5%) got as much as Tshs[††]. 4,000 (about ` 123) a day, while about 28% got between Tshs. 4,001 and 6,000, 23.1% got between Tshs. 6,001 and 10,000 and the last group (17.7%) got above Tshs 10,000.

Daily earning and needs

The catch of the begging is instant money and money only in exchange of nothing or a few words of pleas. But in larger social context money comes to beggars at a very heavy price for this money. They have to face stigma, shame, dishonour, self-prestige loss and so on.

Table 2.15: Daily Income of the respondents

Earnings	No. of Respondents	Percentage
Up to 100	21	42
101 – 200	14	28
201 – 300	9	18
301 and above	6	12
Total	**50**	**100**

On question of daily income by begging beggars gave different responses. Twenty-one (42%) respondents said that they earn less than `

[††] 1 Tanzanian Shilling (Tsh) equals 0.031 Indian Rupee

100. Fourteen (28%) said that they earn between ` 101 to 200. Nine (18%) said that they earn between ` 201 to 300 and six (12%) beggars said that they earn more than ` 300 a day. Women and disabled person make more money than other type of beggars. It is further observed that people who beg daily and are more experienced earn a little more money than newcomers. Skills are developed in finding a location or choosing a time of day and how to approach potential givers. In a study by Alison Murdoch[76] it was found that the public are more likely to give to extrovert, even cheeky people than to those sitting quietly on pavements (or any place).

Jhoot kya bolna, kareeb 300 tak ban jata hai din ka… Itna bi na bne to kaise guzara chelga bheek mangne se. kabhi kam bi milta hai kabi zyada… kharcha pura ho jata hai mera… [Telling frankly (not lie), I earn about ` 300 daily… If one could not earn even this much amount how could one survive on begging. Sometime (I) get less, sometime more… (I get) enough to meet my (daily) expenses].

Table 2.16: Whether satisfied with earnings

Satisfaction	No. of Respondents	Percentage
Not Satisfied	12	24
Somewhat Satisfied	20	40
Fully Satisfied	18	36
Total	**50**	**100**

Regarding their daily income in begging, it was asked from beggars that whether they were satisfied from their income? To which twelve (24%) beggars said that they were not satisfied with their income as it became very tough for them to meet all the expenses of daily life. However, twenty (40%) beggars said that they were somewhat satisfied. *"Zyada mil jata to acha hota lekin itne mein bhi kaam chal jata hai"* [It would be better if I get more but I can manage even with whatever I get]. Eighteen (36%) beggars said that they were fully satisfied with their daily earnings, these were the ones who earn more than ` 200 or have other earning members in the family.

Table 2.17: Other sources of income

Other Sources	No. of Respondents	Percentage
Yes	8	16
No	42	84
Total	**50**	**100**

Forty-two (84%) beggar respondents said that they have no other source of income other than begging while eight (16%) said that they have other source too like land in their village etc. However, their family members are engaged in range of activities from begging & labourer to Mechanic etc.

"Aur kuch ni karta, kuch aur sadhan se paise mil jate to bheek kyun mangta… Na zameen hai apni aur na kuch kaam kr sta hun bas maang ke hi guzara chalta hai apna". [I don't do any other work except begging, If I had other source of income then why should I beg…I don't own any land and unable to do any other work, Begging is my only source of livelihood].

Table 2.18: Saving for future

Saving	No. of Respondents	Percentage
Yes	31	62
No	9	18
Sometimes	10	20
Total	**50**	**100**

Thirty-one (62%) beggar respondents said that they save their money for future as it is uncertain when they need money. They save for marriages, disease, for future security. Nine (18%) respondents said that they do not save money and spent all they earn. And ten (20%) respondents said that when they earn more money they save it otherwise they spend most money on their basic daily needs. Those who save money said that they even have bank accounts where they can save without any threat of being stolen or cheating.

Jhuggi mein kya pta kb paisa chori ho jaye ya kon paise utha le... is liye Bank mein rakh deta hun... [You never know when you get robbed in a *jhuggi* or when someone take your money... That's why I use to save money in bank].

Therefore, it was observed that though, they were illiterate but were aware of certain things like, opening bank account for their economic security.

Through socio-cultural and economic profile of beggars, one can now easily understand their living and working conditions, their lifestyle and will further help in understanding their problems in detail. By looking at their socio-economic profile, one can even observe how culture of poverty as well as social exclusion prevails among them.

NOTES

58 Bryan S. Turner. 2006. *The Cambridge Dictionary of Sociology*. New York: Cambridge University Press.

59 Steve Bruce and Steven Yearley. 2006. *The Sage Dictionary of Sociology*. London: SAGE Publications.

60 Op. cit. Ref. 1.

61 Karl Marx. 1843. *Critique of Hegel's Philosophy of Right*. Translated by Annette Jolin and Joseph O'Malley. Cambridge: Cambridge University Press. Accessed May 06, 2015. https://www.marxists.org/archive/marx/works/1843/critique-hpr/index.htm.

62 Nicholas Abercrombie, Stephen Hill, and Bryan S. Turner. 1984. *The Penguin Dictionary of Sociology*. London: Penguin Books.

63 Sonia Malik, and Sanjoy Roy. 2012. "A Study on Begging: A Social Stigma-An Indian Perspective." *Journal of Human Values* 18 (2): 187-199. doi:10.1177/0971685812454486.

64 Tara Patel. 1959. "Some Reflections of the Beggar Problem in Ahmedabad." *Sociological Bulletin* 8 (1): 5-15. Accessed September 30, 2015. http://www.jstor.org/stable/42864545.

65 David Shichor, and Ruth Ellis. 1981. "Begging in Israel: An exploratory study." *Deviant Behavior* 2 (2): 109-125. doi:10.1080/01639625.1981.9967546.

66 Op. cit. Ref. 7.

67 Registrar General and Census Commision. n.d. "Concepts and Definitions." *Census of India*. Accessed June 11, 2016. http://censusindia.gov.in/Data_Products/Data_Highlights/Data_Highlights_link/concepts_def_hh.pdf.

68 Madhav Sadashiv Gore. 1958. "Society and the Beggar." *Sociological Bulletin* 7 (1): 23-48. Accessed September 30, 2015. http://www.jstor.org/stable/42864528.

69 Baltazar M.L. Namwata, and Maseke R. Mgabo. 2012. "Feelings of Beggars on Begging Life and their Survival Livelihoods in Urban Areas of Central Tanzania." *International Journal of Physical and Social Sciences (IJPSS)* 2 (7). Accessed December 20, 2015. http://www.ijmra.us/project%20doc/IJPSS_JULY2012/IJMRA-PSS1401.pdf.

70 Ibid.

71 Ibid.

72 Op. cit. Ref. 7.

[73] *Greater Kashmir.* 2016. "Liquor consumption increases in J&K." June 1. Accessed June 2, 2016. http://www.greaterkashmir.com/news/kashmir/liquor-consumption-increases-in-j-k/219154.html.

[74] Op. cit. Ref. 6.

[75] Op. cit. Ref. 12.

[76] Alison Murdoch, Liz Connell, Jean Davis, and Joanne Maher. 1994. *We are human too: a study of people who beg.* London: Crisis.

3: THE BEGGARY PROBLEM: REASONS OF BEGGING AND STATE'S RESPONSE

Begging is the last of last resort for survival and livelihood. Even if one is poor, s/he tries to improve his/her conditions by continuously doing some kind of work. Becoming a beggar means, that particular person has failed as a member of larger society (as he/she is indulged in a deviant/illegal activity). He has reduced himself to 'nobody' for other members of society who earns their livelihood through some kind of productive work. Living in society implies that people have social bonds with other members of the society (within their own group as well as outside it) and hold some prestige and self-esteem. They do not want to beg because they fear of a loss of these things, which are of prime importance in their social life. Yet, one finds people begging in almost every city and town. What makes them beggar? Of course, they are poor but aren't there so many poor who do not beg? Is beggar a deviant poor or a lazy fellow?

This chapter has highlighted some major reasons of begging and various other associated aspects to understand these reasons. This chapter has also focused its attention on legal perspective on begging and the State's response towards begging. Before discussing these major themes of the chapter, below are some associated aspects on the background information of beggars, to understand their presence in begging.

BEGGING CAREER

Shichor and Ellis (1981)[77] argued that most people started begging in places where there exists a large daily turnover of people. However, after getting somewhat accustomed to their new trade (attitudinal adjustment) and after learning the basic techniques of begging, they start to look for other locations, mainly because of the "bad companionship" of other beggars at their present location. Most of them start begging after being engaged previously in some type of work. In most cases, it was a gradual process, similar to what Becker (1963)[78] described as the "sequential model of deviant careers." In several cases it started by receiving and accepting charity from a synagogue (Jews' religious place). After a while recipients reasoned that if it is acceptable to receive charity from a synagogue, it is also acceptable to ask for and receive money from pedestrians. In other cases, after making a few futile attempts to find permanent positions in their previous trades and working on and off in temporary jobs, some of them became street vendors and gradually started begging. Most of them suffered a strain-producing period in the face of high unemployment, housing shortages, and other problems. Shichor and Ellis (1981) further discussed the process of people getting into begging and their begging career – Some beggars reported that they arrived at the begging solution by themselves without any advice or encouragement from anyone else. One woman reported that she started begging after seeing some people in her neighbourhood doing the same. A blind beggar was introduced to begging by members of his family. In many respects their "career development" resembled that of the "social and economic failures" described by Gilmore; they were mainly people who experienced a downward socioeconomic mobility that they could not control. One of the older beggars, in their study, was still in the process of becoming a beggar. According to his account he used to sit on a bench near a synagogue, and one day, without this having asked, people started to give him money. Since then he came regularly to the same location and solicited quietly. When people known to him came by, he stopped soliciting and sat quietly on the bench. Some respondents pointed out that they felt more comfortable working at their permanent post than somewhere else where nobody knew them, because it was "unpleasant" for them to ask for charity in "strange" places. Most of them, however, stated that they would be embarrassed to beg in their own neighbourhood. A few beggars had exclusive private posts. They secured them at the busiest places of the city and scared away their competitors by cursing them loudly, by appealing to the public not to give money to the intruder, and often also by using connections with municipal supervisors who know them.

In Jammu beggars have also similar tales about their begging career. Most beggars here too, came to begging after changing various professions of lower or deviant nature. Some however have directly started begging after being raised up in culture of poverty. At initial stage of begging they faced some problems while interacting with people and in getting adequate money from them. But gradually, as they got experienced, they were then used to it and also made more money. As discussed earlier most of the beggars in Jammu are migrants from neighbouring states. They prefer to beg in strange (where no one know about them) places. This is because there is a shame attached to begging so they beg away from their hometowns so that no one (among persons who know him/her) could recognise them. Before discussing the reasons of begging let us look at different aspects on the background information about the beggars to better understand their reasons of begging.

Duration (Time) in Begging

Duration or time period in begging is helpful to ascertain whether begging is a short term activity or relatively longer or permanent one.

Table 3.1: Duration in Begging

Years in Begging	No. of Respondents	Percentage
Below 5	22	44
6-15	18	36
16-30	6	12
31 and above	4	8
Total	**50**	**100**

From the above table it is clear that 22 (44%) respondents were in begging for a time period of 5 years or less. Eighteen (36%) beggar respondents were in this activity for a time period of 6-15 years, six (12%) for 16-30 years and four (8%) beggars were begging for 31 years are above. Most of them believed that begging has now become a part of their life as they have become habitual to it. However, some of the respondents who were in begging for less than 5 years said that it was a transitory phase and wished to leave begging if they could get some alternative work.

Age at the time of start of the Begging

It is to denote at what stage (phase) of life respondents started begging.

Table 3.2: Age at which the respondents started begging

Age at start of the Begging	No. of Respondents	Percentage
18 and below	5	10
19-30	9	18
31-50	22	44
51 and above	14	28
Total	**50**	**100**

From above table it is found that five (10%) beggars started begging at age of 18 years or less. Nine (18%) respondents started begging at age of 19-30 years. While most respondents i.e., Twenty-two (44%) said that they started begging at age of 31-50 years, fourteen (28%) respondents said that they came into begging at later stage of life i.e., 51 years or above (as active employment seeking age, especially for those with no formal education, i.e. 15-24 years),[79] only about 28% respondents started begging before attaining the age of 30 years. Among these 28%, were mostly hereditary beggars and other individuals who have left their families or had no family. While other 72% (44+28) started begging after the age of 30 due to various reason discussed in this chapter.

Occupation of the Parents of the Beggars

To better understand the background of the families of beggar respondents, question about occupation of their parents were asked from them. It was found that beggars who were begging in Jammu city had come from different family backgrounds.

Table 3.3: Occupation of the Parents of the Beggars respondents

Occupation of Parents	No of Beggars	Percentage
Farmer/Farm Labourer	12	24
Labourer	10	20
Beggar	8	16
Barber	1	2
Sweeper	3	6
Govt. Job	2	4
Priest	1	2
Others	5	10
No Response	8	16
Total	**50**	**100**

From the above table it was found that parents (in majority cases refers to father) of twelve (24%) beggars were farmers or farm labourers by occupation, ten (20%) were labourers, eight (16%) were beggars, one (2%) was Barber, three (6%) were sweepers, two (4%) were in some government jobs, while one (2%) said that his father was priest in a temple. Further there were eight (16%) respondents who either do not know their parent's occupation or refused to tell and five (10%) said that their parents changed various occupation and thus listed as others. Except a few, parental occupation of most of the respondents falls in lower class in modern societies. The ones whose parents were in Government job, were engaged in class IVth jobs (like peon etc.) and were no more with them (died). The data also signifies that beggars did not belong to lower class strata only (like poverty) but were spread across different castes.

Respondent's Occupation before starting begging

Table 3.4: Occupation of respondents before coming into begging

Occupation	No. of Respondents	Percentage
No Occupation earlier	13	26
Labourer	16	32
Kabaddi	5	18
Farm Labourer	6	8
Worked in Hotel	2	4
Job	1	2
Other Works	6	6
No Response	2	4
Total	**50**	**100**

What a beggar did before he start begging? Did he do something else earlier or directly started begging. In the present study thirteen (26%) respondents said that they directly started begging without doing any other work. However, the remaining respondents said that they were in some other works/occupations or jobs before coming into begging. Sixteen (32%) said that they were labourers prior to joining begging, five (10%) were kabaddis, six (12%) were agricultural labourers, two (4%) worked in hotel, one (2%) beggar said he had some government job (contractual), six (12%) said they tried different jobs and categorised as others while two (4%) did not answered satisfactorily. Thus majority of the respondents were either labourer or had no work before coming into begging. Shichor and Ellis (1981),[80] also observed in their study that the occupational background of the beggars was such that they had very low prestige in modern society and same was the case with respondents in present study.

REASONS OF BEGGING

To understand begging, one should have the understanding of its reasons and causes. As discussed earlier begging is an ambiguous, complex and controversial activity. Different persons beg for various different reasons or situational forces. Moreover, there cannot be a single reason which can explain why an individual beg but (a combination of) multiple reasons.

As B.B. Pande (1986)[81] believed that generally, social parasitism (begging) is inspired by any of three motivations:

i) by economic necessity resulting from extreme resourcelessness and destitution;

ii) by the altruistic spirit based on religious or traditional considerations as in the case of *sadhu, sanyasi, darvesh* and *fakir*, and

iii) hedonistic considerations designed to avoid the drudgery of hard work and industry.

Anderson (1961)[82] has classified reasons of begging as unemployment and seasonal work; the misfits (physical disabled) of industry; defects of personality; crisis in the life of the person; racial or national discrimination and wanderlust.

Tara Patel (1959)[83] in a study in Ahamedabad summarised the reasons of begging as: i) Poverty, Unsupported, unemployed, part-time beggars ii) Habitual Beggars iii) Physically handicapped, mentally retarded, diseased iv) Cruelty of relatives v) To live a care free life vi) Fatalist vii) Shameful remorse for his incestuous relation viii) Helped to live as prostitute.

She argued that in majority of the cases the driving force is economic. Besides the majority of beggars who have referred to economic strains as having been responsible for dragging them into beggary, some of the disabled and diseased could not have been drawn into this profession if adequate means to engage them in gainful occupation were in existence. While economic factor was the driving force, hereditary begging is equally staggering. She found that one fifth of the total respondents were hereditary beggars.

I. General Reasons of Begging

The general reasons as cited by beggars themselves during fieldwork and also discussed by various earlier studies are briefly discussed as follows:

Destitution (Extreme Poverty): Whether fraud or genuine, all beggars at some point face extreme poverty (usually before they start begging) which push them towards begging. Poverty is general scarcity, dearth, or the state of one who lacks a usual or socially acceptable amount of money or material possessions.[84] It is a multifaceted concept, which includes social, economic, and political elements. Poverty may be defined as either absolute or relative. Absolute poverty or destitution refers to the lack of means necessary to meet basic needs such as food, clothing and shelter. Relative poverty takes into consideration individual social and economic status compared to the rest of society. In context of begging it is absolute poverty, in majority of cases, which become a reason for people to beg.

In present study about 80% respondents said that poverty (in respondent's sense and not as defined by government or any government agency) was one of the main reason which made them beggars. In absolute poverty (destitution), people don't have much choices of choosing among different occupations or career options, they grab whatever come in their way. *"Us din mere pass ek paise bi nahin bacha tha kuch samajh ni lg rha tha ke kya karon… Bazzar gaya aur mangne lga logon se…"* [That day I was left with no money, I could not understand what to do… I went to market and started begging from people].

Murdoch (1994)[85] also highlighted upon poverty as one of the reason of begging. He asked people during his study that what set them on the road to begging. The most obvious answer came "I only do it when I'm short of money. Lack of money makes you beg." However more detailed patterns did emerge. Half of the people asked this question highlighted their need for 'basics' using words like 'desperation' and 'survival' and spoke of being hungry and cold. *"I had nothing to eat, no money and I wanted some tea. That was the first time I begged from others."*

Unemployment: Unemployment occurs when people who are without work are actively seeking paid work. The unemployment rate is a measure of the prevalence of unemployment and it is calculated as a percentage by dividing the number of unemployed individuals by all individuals currently in the labour force. According to International Labour Organization report, more than 200 million people globally or 6% of the world's workforce were without a job in 2012.[86] Marx (1863)[87] argued that it is in the very nature of the capitalist mode of production to overwork some workers while keeping the rest as a reserve army of unemployed paupers. Some studies highlighted that Unemployment, instead of poverty, is the main reason of begging.

About 50% respondents in present study cited unemployment as one of the reasons for getting into begging. Some of them said they had only two options for livelihood (other than criminal activities), i.e., either begging or manual labour and they choose begging over manual work as they were unable to do such works which requires physical strength because of their disability, weakness or illness. Thus, these beggars choose begging as a job (work). One physically handicapped respondent said *"Kaam taalash krna lga to kisi se pta chala ke hum jaise garibon ke liye do hi kaam hote hain, dehari lgao ya bheek maango. Dehari lga ni sakta tha to bheek maangna shru kar diya."* [When I was in search of employment (work) I came to know from someone that poor people like us have only two options – either begging or manual labour work. As I was unable to do manual labour work (due to disability), I started begging]. A small observation was noted during fieldwork when a female beggar was soliciting money from peole in a matador. One person said *"Bheek mangna band karo, jao kuch kaam karo."* [Stop begging around, go find yourself some other work]. To which female beggar replied, *"Tu dega mujhe kaam? lga de kaam pe, chhode dungi mangna"*. [Will you give me a job (work)? If you give me a job, I will stop begging]. The person did not respond any further, the beggar smiled and left the matador.

Murdoch (1994)[88] also observed that some people (in his study) started begging because of the loss of or lack of a job. *"Begging is something to get me money until I can find something else – a job... a proper job with decent wages."*

Illiteracy and lack of Skills: Literacy is traditionally understood as the ability to read, write, and use arithmetic. The modern term's meaning has been expanded to include the ability to use language, numbers, images, computers, and other basic means to understand, communicate, gain useful knowledge and use the dominant symbol systems of a culture.[89] According to the UNESCO[90], "Literacy involves a continuum of learning in enabling individuals to achieve their goals to develop their knowledge and potential and to participate fully in their community and wider society". Thus, people who lack literacy are illiterates. According to a report by the UNESCO, India has the highest population of illiterate adults at 287 million. This is 37 per cent of the global total. While India's literacy rate rose from 48 per cent in 1991 to 63 per cent in 2006, population growth cancelled the gains so there was no change in the number of illiterate adults.

Illiteracy is also one of the major reason of begging especially that of hereditary beggars. In the present study, it was found that most of the respondents (86%) were illiterates. In modern societies, every job requires some knowledge or some skills which can only be obtained through formal education or practical training. Lack of education hinders individuals' chances of acquiring skills and ultimately of getting a good job and thus exposes him to hard jobs like labour work or other deviant activity like begging. Surplus of unskilled labour force them to earn their livelihood through any means even if it may be considered deviant by wider society.

Disability: According to World Health Organisation[91], Disability is an umbrella term, covering impairments, activity limitations, and participation restrictions. An impairment is a problem in body function or structure; an activity limitation is a difficulty encountered by an individual in executing a task or action; while a participation restriction is a problem experienced by an individual in involvement in life situations. Thus, disability is a complex phenomenon, reflecting an interaction between features of a person's body and features of the society in which he or she lives.

Disability restricts the individual's activities which he/she can do for his/her livelihood. It is very tough for a disabled person to get a job and even if he/she get one, it is also tough to manage it. Most of the beggars are disabled destitute with unemployment and no family support. Twenty-two (44%) beggars in the present study were physically handicapped and cited disability was the major reason which left them with no other option but to beg. *"Jab haath pavon hi na hoon bhaiya to aur kya kaam kr skte hain… Khane keliye kisi tarah kammana to padega"* [When one doesn't have hands and legs, what else he can do…For livelihood one has to earn, by any means].

Hereditary Occupation: Some beggar respondents (16%) are pursuing begging as their hereditary (family) occupation. They were in begging because of the fact that their parents were also doing the same and they are simply continuing their family tradition. In India where there was a tradition of pursuing hereditary occupations (caste groups were categorised on the basis of occupation), there were various castes which were beggars by occupation i.e., in division of labour they were assigned to beg only. Remaining in poverty and begging has become a subculture for these type of groups. So they are living in and perpetuating what Lewis termed as 'Culture of poverty', a cycle of poverty. However, it was clear from the table 3.3 (on occupation of beggar's parents) that many beggars did not have begging as their hereditary occupation and their parents were engaged in different occupation (though of low status comparatively).

Influence of Others: Some respondents said that they came into begging after some of their friends (who were also beggars) suggested or persuaded them to do so. Some of them said that they saw their neighbour begging so they also started begging. A few also said that initially they were forced into begging against their will, mostly likely by their guardians. As of one female beggar (also quoted earlier in chapter 2), "*She* (referring to her mother-in-law; married at 13) *initially beat me when I refused to go for begging as at that time I really hated begging…*" Thus influence of others is also a factor contributing to begging.

In Murdoch's (1994)[92] study too, some beggars said they had started begging because of the influence of friends. Usually this was in the context of homelessness and shortage of money. *"(It was) just being homeless. I didn't want to sponge. I just wanted to sort myself out – get a flat. Then I got in with the wrong people."*

Weakness and Prolonged Illness: Eight (16%) respondents said that it was due to their physical weakness, due to old age or prolonged illness that has restricted their options of doing some other works. Among them some said, before being physically weak they were engaged in some other works and left after they were not able to continue any further. *"60 saal tak Kabadi ka kaam kiya, jab zoor kam hua to kam krne mein mushkil hone lgi… uske bad bheek mangna shuru ki"* [For 60 years I worked as *Kabadi* (rag-picker), then due to physical weakness it was tough to continue my work… After that I started begging].

Easy Job: In begging, beggars get money easily as compared to any other work or occupation. It is an occupation of only getting money directly from the people without any interference of third party like - boss, employer or middleman. Moreover, in this job no physical efforts are required not even any special skills. One has to just plead for money from other people. This is the main reason which explains why if one starts one cannot leave it easily.

Stones (2013)[93] points out that the most common problem is that beggars are so used to begging that they actually prefer not to work. Many of them also make more money from begging than they would if they did work. Continuing with this notion that an individual's circumstances tend to lead to the practice of begging, it is further noted that for many, begging is a more acceptable means of satisfying immediate needs than resorting to… criminal activity such as theft, drug dealing or prostitution.

In present study in Jammu city, though, respondents did not cite this reason but from their different reasons, it can be said that apart from other conditions which forced people into begging, it's easy (no hard work as a job) nature also played some role in attracting people.

Isolation and failed aspirations: Socially isolated or alienated people are much prone to begging, as they had no known persons in front of whom they could feel shame (because of begging), and also they have no social relationships who can support them financially or encourage them to achieve higher status. There were some cases of individuals who had left their families for career and after failing in their career, they become extremely isolated and took to begging. Following two news stories from India's leading newspaper "The Times of India" illustrate this point:

A dream shattered: Cops find starlet begging and stealing (The Times of

India Apr 26, 2016)[94]: "Police have found a starlet begging and stealing on the roads of Lokhandwala. Mitali Sharma, 25, took to begging after her career stalled and her parents abandoned her for pursuing her dreams of becoming an actor. Sharma told the cops that she has acted in a Bhojpuri film, that she snagged a couple of modelling assignments and that she slipped into depression after her career stalled."

Gita's story: From ramp model to beggar (The Times of India Sep 4, 2007)[95]: "In the '90s, Gitanjali Nagpal sashayed down the catwalks of Delhi with the likes of Sushmita Sen. A Navy officer's daughter who went to Lady Shri Ram College, she seemed set for a flashbulb career in fashion. On Sunday, they found her living off the streets and spending her nights in parks and temples and getting money from people by begging."

In Jammu city too, some beggar respondents said that they were in begging because of isolation and disappointment from life, as one beggar said 'my wife has deserted me, I felt lonely and lost interest in life… then I started begging.

Disruptive Family or Breakdown of family: Disruptive family background refers to the problems or abuse they had faced in their families. Beggar respondents with disruptive family background had experienced physical, mental or sexual abuse, violence and harassment from their family members so they had left that family and started begging.

Some beggars also faced family breakdown due to death of their family head (or person on whom they were economically dependent) or separation which triggered them to begging like some orphans and widows. Murdoch (1994)[96] is also of the view that relationship breakdown had set them on the road to begging. "(My) *marital home dissolved. I didn't have anywhere to go. I didn't know anyone else in the city… I thought it was better than thieving and stealing and violently robbing people.*"

Low self-esteem: Whatever reason may push or pull people into begging (destitution, unemployment, easy job or heredity) one thing will be associated with all, i.e., they all have low self-esteem or low self-regard. As begging is highly stigmatised activity and people in this activity have a very low status as compared to larger society.

Fun: According to Murdoch (1994)[97], a few people referred to fun as an incentive but then added that the fun had worn off. *"All I wanted to do was get loaded and have a good time… now it sucks, it's not my trip. There has been a change in me and in people's attitudes to beggars… If I got a flat tomorrow I wouldn't need to beg again."* However, in present study also there was one beggar who said initially he came into begging for fun but after some time, he became habitualised to it and preferred it other over works.

Alcohol or Drugs: Various reports also suggests that people also beg for their addiction for alcohol and drugs. These report put forth that many people are addicted to alcohol and some other expensive drugs. To fulfil their addiction need they need money; and when they are short of money and in addicted state they don't bother even to beg. In present study also 62% beggars admitted that they use alcohol but also maintained that it is not the cause of their begging but they rather take it to feel relaxed and enjoy for sometimes after the day-long work. In Murdoch's study some people specifically mentioned that they needed money for alcohol or drugs: *"Skint and broke and needed a drink. I didn't actually like it, but with a few cans in me what's the difference."*

On the Run: A few studies also suggest (although no respondents cited this reason in present study) that there are a few people who beg because they run away from their native places after indulging in some crime or other such activity. They are on the run from police and thus prefer absolute anonymity which only begging can provide to them.

II. Macro-Level Reasons for Begging

These general reasons of why people beg or why begging exists any society, can be broadly categorised into following four major categories:

Social Exclusion (Structural)

Social exclusion is a multidimensional concept that not only embraces income poverty but also encompasses deprivation across social, economic and political spheres of life. It is concerned with the processes that sustain disadvantage.[98] Social exclusion involves the lack or denial of resources, rights, goods and services, and the inability to participate in the normal relationships and activities, available to the majority of people in a society, whether in economic, social, cultural or political arenas. It affects both the quality of life of individuals and the equity and cohesion of society as a whole. (Mack 2016)[99] Apart from poverty and discrimination, social exclusion results in degradation of one's self-esteem. After loss of one's self esteem it is not difficult for anyone to start begging. One can therefore, argue that beggars are the marginal within the marginalised who are socially excluded because of their material conditions and also due to their culture (ways of living).

Culture of Poverty

The culture of poverty is a concept in social theory that expands on the idea of a cycle of poverty. It offers one way to explain why poverty exists despite anti-poverty programs. Early proponents of the theory argued that the poor are not only lacking resources but also acquire a poverty-perpetuating value system[100]. According to anthropologist Oscar Lewis, "The subculture [of the poor] develops mechanisms that tend to perpetuate it, especially because of what happens to the worldview, aspirations, and character of the children who grow up in it." The term "subculture of poverty" (later shortened to "culture of poverty") made its first appearance in Lewis's ethnography *Five Families: Mexican Case Studies in the Culture of Poverty* (1959)[101]. He argued that although the burdens of poverty were systemic and so imposed upon these members of society, they led to the formation of an autonomous subculture as children were socialized into behaviours and attitudes that perpetuated their inability to escape the underclass.

Lewis (1998)[102] gave 70 characteristics that indicated the presence of the culture of poverty, which he argued was not shared among all of the lower classes.

The people in the culture of poverty have a strong feeling of marginality, of helplessness, of dependency, of not belonging. They are like aliens in their own country, convinced that the existing institutions do not serve their interests and needs. Along with this feeling of powerlessness is a widespread feeling of inferiority, of personal unworthiness. People with a culture of poverty have very little sense of history. They are a marginal people who know only their own troubles, their own local conditions, their own neighbourhood, their own way of life. Usually, they have neither the knowledge, the vision nor the ideology to see the similarities between their problems and those of others like themselves elsewhere in the world. In other words, they are not class conscious, although they are very sensitive indeed to status distinctions. When the poor become class conscious or members of trade union organizations, or when they adopt an internationalist outlook on the world they are, in my view, no longer part of the culture of poverty although they may still be desperately poor. - (Lewis, The Culture of Poverty 1998)

The beggars in Jammu exhibit culture of poverty as evident from the discussions made above and in chapter 2.

Society's Encouragement

Religious alms giving tradition: All religions of the world encourage alms giving to the poor and needy, by all such individuals who can do so - like *Zakat* (in Muslims) and *Daan* (in Hinduism). This religious emphasis on alms-giving tradition serve to socially and financially legitimize beggary. Although beggars are discouraged and hated by most of the people in any society but they still exist as they have backing of a religious tradition. This is why one sees most people beg in the name of God, Allah, and Bhagwan etc. Alms-giving tradition was seen in Jammu also. Jammu is known as city of temples and people here strongly believed in alms-giving tradition which can be regarded as one of the major factor that encourage and perpetuates begging.

Pity for the vulnerable is the key in widespread of begging. Helping the vulnerable or destitute and needy is a value in society. As one disabled beggar respondent discussed his first begging encounter, *"Mein hospital ke bahar betha hua tha, ek aadmi aaya aur ek rupayaa rakh diya mere aage fir aur aaya aur wo bi paise dene lage. Tab mujhi laga ki yahi kaam karna padega paise kamane keliye aur meine bheek mangna shuru kar diya..."* [I was sitting outside the hospital, a stranger came and give me a coin then some more followed. That was the moment I realised that this is the way for me to earn my livelihood and I started begging from people...].

Religious traditions and People's compassion for beggars encourages individuals to become beggars. As they are in dire need of money and find begging as an easy way of earning money irrespective of their physical and metal traits. In this way, structural forces of a society are also responsible for widespread of beggary.

Beggar's Needs (Individual)

In most of the cases they do not choose it of their own free will but they are forced into it. Some are forced into begging by others, some are forced by their economic or social condition, and still others are forced by their own culture. In short their need force them into begging. These needs factor (discussed earlier in this chapter) are therefore:

Economic (Poverty, Unemployment, Earn surplus income); *Social* (Caste, Illiteracy, Disruptive/No family); *Cultural* (Hereditary Occupation); *Biological* (Old age, Sickness/Disease, Physical Disability)

Thus, people beg for different reasons. Reasons listed above are the major ones due to which people come into begging. Here, one can argue that almost all these conditions/situations listed above as reasons for begging are (or could be) faced by majority of population in our country but not everyone is a beggar. The difference between a normal poor and a beggar is mainly due to deviance, low self-esteem, lack of proper information and urgency. However, there cannot be only a single reason for which a person comes into begging, rather, a combination of different reasons simultaneously becomes a cause of begging. For Example – poverty along with unemployment and disability; Hereditary occupation and unemployment: Disruptive family background and low self-esteem, and so on.

When respondents were asked about the reason of begging in Jammu they gave reasons like -Jammu is away from their hometowns, so they beg here (away from home) as most of them argued that they felt ashamed of begging in their home city. Some respondents said that they chose Jammu as they had earlier visited here and after getting into begging, they preferred to beg in Jammu. Among them some respondents came for pilgrimage to *Mata Vaishno Devi* while others said that they came to Jammu in search of work but later started begging and settled here. A few physically handicapped respondents said that they beg here because other people (some friends or relatives) from their hometowns were already working here (most of whom are labourers) and suggested/persuaded them to come here.

However, most of the respondents believed that people in Jammu are more religious and generous as compared to other places where they begged earlier, which helped them in getting good alms here. Beggar respondents believed that people here pity or vulnerable (like beggars). One beggar, when asked about his opinion on, why people give alms (money) to him, he responded *"Hamari halat dekh ke taras aa jata hai logon ko aur de jate hain kuch paise"* [On seeing our condition people feels pity for us and give some change].

SATISFACTION IN BEGGING AS WORK

Almost all the beggars, in the present study, argued that at some point of time (during working as beggar) they disliked and even hated begging (mostly in initial stage), but when they realised that they are unfit for any other job or unable to get any job, some of them started liking it. Some beggars still hate begging but they too have learned to adapt to the situation gradually. Whether they are satisfied or not but they have realised that they are 'beggars'.

Stones (2013)[103] argued that this belief of having a lack of skills to do anything else introduces an element that is of particular interest, namely, the idea of people resorting to begging because they have a limited self-concept or poor self-regard. Moreover, with the passage of time, it tends to become increasingly difficult for someone engaged in street begging (regardless of their initial level of self-esteem) to view themselves as being capable of doing anything different from their current activities, or to imagine alternative ways of being and earning a living. Stones (2013) further discussed the satisfaction in panhandling by noting beggar's responses on, whether begging is pleasing activity? To which *43% participants replied "yes," commonly because of the opportunity to "meet people," 48% answered "no," often describing panhandling as "degrading," and 9% were undecided. Overall, 70% stated that they would prefer a minimum-wage job, typically citing a desire for a "steady income" or "getting off the street."* However, many felt they could not handle conventional jobs because of mental illness, physical disability or lack of skills.

Choice to Stay in or Leave Begging

Would beggars leave begging if provided a chance? Why? For what alternative? These were the questions which were explored during research, to look into their choice.

Table 3.5: Choice to stay in or leave begging

Leave Begging	No. of Respondents	Percentage
No	11	22
Yes	35	70
Uncertain	4	8
Total	**50**	**100**

Respondents, in the present study, were asked whether they would like to leave begging if they were given a chance. To which 70% replied 'Yes", 22% said 'No' and 8% were 'Uncertain'. Those who said that they would like to leave begging were ready to do so only when they could get some alternative work or economic help. Some of them said that they would be happy to leave begging if they could get any work in which earning is equivalent or more than what they get in begging or any government job with good salary. Some were ready to leave if given other jobs like that of Watchman, Salesman in shop, or any work which do not require much physical strength. A few said that they can even do manual labour work if they would get wages on time.

Malik and Roy (2012)[104] also observed that the statement that 'Begging is a shame for the beggars and they want to quit' seems to hold true seeing the statistics. A good number of the people (71 per cent) in this profession do not really like their work. Majority (64 per cent) of the beggars are ready to quit if work is available with 42 per cent of them ready to do so for a meagre monthly income of 3,000 per month, whereas 32 per cent of them expect an income of more than 6,000 per month.

Patel (1959),[105] in her study, argued that when beggars were asked whether they were ready to give up beggary if other means of subsistence would be provided, more than half of them positively refused to give up, questioning why they should give it up when people were ready to give them alms, one third of the total respondents verbally showed their willingness to give up beggary if other means of subsistence were provided to them. In spite of this, only about 12% beggars may be said to be keen about getting a job in preference to begging. They considered begging humiliating to them. They also believed that they were debtors to the people from whom they received alms and shall have to repay the debt in their next birth. 11% beggars were ready to give up begging if they were offered jobs of their own choice. Some were not prepared to leave begging because they said that they led a carefree life and that they did not want any bondage or social restrictions.

STATE'S RESPONSE TOWARDS BEGGING

The beggar issue is in the jurisdiction of "National Institute of Social Defence," a subordinate autonomous body under the Ministry of Social Justice & Empowerment. It is the nodal training and research institute in the field of social defence. Social defence covers the entire gamut of activities and programmes for the protection of society like "drug abuse prevention, welfare of senior citizens, *beggary prevention,* transgender and other social defence issues". It views on begging are as - "Beggary is serious problem in India which needs to be addressed on priority. Laws against vagrancy and beggary are a means of control over such persons, who constitute a source of potential threat and annoyance to society".[106] This view on beggary by a government agency indicates how government look at beggars. Instead of viewing them as socially excluded and vulnerable destitute in need of help from the government (welfare State), they are seen as potential threat and annoyance to society.

Beggars are non-political entities as there is no lobbying for them in political sphere. They are looked upon as parasites especially by government. Due to the fact that beggars lack political power they are mostly ignored in government welfare schemes for the poor instead they are criminalised (as act of begging is an offence in most of states in India).

Criminalising Begging

In the initial stages beggary and vagrancy were not seen as serious social problems. They were, at best, considered minor deviations on the part of the surplus labour population pending their full employment. The history of criminalising beggars is as old as of 1349, when first regulation with respect to prohibition of begging was passed in England with the title of 'English Statue of Labourers, 1349'. Its basic purpose was to increase the workforce following the 'Black Death'[‡‡] by making 'idleness' (unemployment) an offence. This law also enacted as at that time it was believed that Jews, lepers, beggars, and foreigners were the cause for the spread of 'Black death' and the government must regulate and control them. This legislation was considered as one of the most draconian law at that time, as the punishment was very severe (Baker 2009)[107].

Beggars were treated with iron hand during that period and aftermath. Although, the needy (genuine beggars) were treated compassionately, there were severe punishments for the sturdy beggars. In 1530, Henry VIII decreed that "beggars who are old and incapable of working receive a beggar's licence. On the other hand, whipping and imprisonment for sturdy vagabonds. They are to be tied to the cart-tail and whipped until the blood streams from their bodies, then they are to swear on oath to go back to their birthplace or to serve where they have lived the last three years and to 'put themselves to labour'. For the second arrest for vagabondage the whipping is to be repeated and half the ear sliced off; but for the third relapse the offender is to be executed as a hardened criminal and enemy of the common weal."[108]

In 1824, earlier vagrancy laws were consolidated in the "Vagrancy Act 1824 (UK)" whose main aim was removing undesirables from public view. The act assumed that homelessness was due to idleness and thus deliberate, and made it a criminal offence to engage in behaviours associated with extreme poverty. The Poor Law was the system for the provision of social security in operation in England and Wales from the 16th century until the establishment of the Welfare State in the 20th century. The Vagrancy Act of 1824 is of prime importance as it is the major act in relation to anti-begging and has been mostly used in all

---

[‡‡] The Black Death was an epidemic of bubonic plague, a disease caused by the bacterium Yersinia pestis that circulates among wild rodents where they live in great numbers and density. It occurred in Europe in 1346-53 and killed about 50 million people or 60% of Europe's total population.

contemporary anti-begging Acts not only in UK but also in India.[109]

Mukherjee (2008)[110] asserts that there is a long history of legal measures against begging. The first legal measure against beggary and vagrancy in India was the European Vagrancy Act, 1874, which was meant to deal with vagrants of European descent. For common people, the general power of prevention of offences security provisions could be launched according to Code of Criminal Procedures (Act V of 1898). Under Section 109 any magistrate was empowered to ask any person without any 'ostensible means of subsistence, or who cannot give a satisfactory account of himself' to execute a bond, with sureties, for good behaviour up to one year. These provisions were used to arrest and detain different undesirable populations and vagabonds. Pande (1986)[111] argued that in India in the early period certain extreme instances of beggary and vagrancy, which adversely affected health, hygiene, decency and morality, were subjected to legal measures stipulated in the Municipalities Acts[112], the Police Acts[113], the Public Nuisance Act[114], etc. Vagrants or beggars were also subjected to various penal provisions under different local acts. The appreciation of beggary and vagrancy as a serious social problem was related crucially with the advent of the capitalist mode of production in India, which led the state to evince greater interest in the control and regulation of these offences through comprehensive formal beggary laws. The handling of the problem of beggary and vagrancy acquired a distinctly formal and penal character in the 1940s when, on account of the post Second World War recession, and the consequent employment freeze and mass retrenchment, the surplus labour force posed a threat to health, the code of decency and to law and order. The first comprehensive penal law relating to beggary and vagrancy was introduced in Bengal in 1943, and was followed by the laws formulated in Mysore (1944), Madras (1945), Bombay (1945) and Kerala (1945). However, after independence, first anti-begging law was enacted by state of Bombay titled as Bombay Prevention of Begging Act (1959) and this act was extended to other states and union territories too.[115]

Dean (1999)[116] argues that in reality, many people found begging, are not prosecuted. While respected sociologists of policing observe that the primary function of the public sector police service has always been to target and control the socially excluded elements of society, among which those found on the streets begging feature prominently, there is, nonetheless, evidence to suggest that many individual police officers have a — often officially sanctioned - tolerant attitude towards those encountered begging on our streets. Intervention and prosecution invariably requires the person to have compounded their actions with aggressive behaviour. He further argues that The evidence of history suggests that more coercive measures have usually been taken against those found begging when the numbers involved visibly escalate and, not surprisingly, this is (notwithstanding the difficulties there are in quantifying the phenomenon) inclined to occur at times of persistent economic recession and social upheaval. At such times, the authorities have tended to favour some form of repressive intervention with the intention of maintaining social order and the protection of the status quo.

Justifications for criminalising begging

The contemporary justifications for criminalising begging and vagrancy centre around two core themes. The first is that vagrancy and begging are a *precursor to more serious crime*. The second focuses on the general offence and nuisance caused to passers-by as a result of the presence of beggars or vagrants (the *public nuisance/ deservedness /intimidation* justification). Baker (2009),[117] in his article discusses the two prominent theories which justifies the anti-beggary laws.

a)   *The "broken windows" justification*

The broken windows theory was proposed by James Q. Wilson and George Kelling in 1982 that used broken windows as a metaphor for disorder within neighbourhoods. Their theory links disorder and incivility within a community to subsequent occurrences of serious crime. The broken windows thesis postulates that there is a nexus between minor incivilities such as begging and more serious crime, once again old laws on begging and vagrancy are being used to target a particular class under the banner of crime prevention. The claims still persist that beggars are tied up in a lot of other crime and that their presence in an area leads to social deprivation and environmental decay, which ultimately induces third parties to commit more serious crime in the affected areas.

b) *Public nuisance and undeserved income justifications*

The second justification that is often raised in support of maintaining begging and vagrancy prohibitions is the umbrage and nuisance that it causes to some passers-by. Robert Ellickson, a professor of law at Yale University, has argued that the public have good reason for finding begging offensive and annoying. Professor Ellickson argues that the sight of idle and allegedly unproductive beggars is enough to cause offence and annoyance to so-called productive people. According to Ellickson, many passers-by resent beggars because they perceive them as unproductive freeloaders. He argues that the public are also offended by begging as people assume that there is a high probability that the beggar's solicitation is fraudulent. However, it is arguable that most passers-by are not so naïve as to assume that the money they give to beggars will not be used for drugs or alcohol in some cases—and as for beggars not paying tax on the money they receive—charitable income is normally tax free. Thus, if people want to give money in these circumstances it hardly makes sense to invoke the criminal law to prevent it. In addition, he suggests that passers-by resent beggars because they are fearful of them.

ANTI-BEGGING LAWS IN INDIA WITH SPECIAL REFERENCE BPBA, 1959

Begging subject is in State list as per Indian Constitution and thus states are authorised to enact on this subject. According to Ministry of Social Justice and Empowerment, "the States are responsible for taking necessary preventive and rehabilitative steps for beggars. As per available data, 20 States and 2 Union Territories have either enacted their own Anti-Beggary Legislation" based on Bombay Prevention of Begging Act (BPBA), 1959. However, shelter homes/ institutions for beggars are functioning only in Gujarat, Karnataka, Madhya Pradesh, Maharashtra, Uttar Pradesh, Uttarakhand, West Bengal and Delhi.

Table 3.6: Existing State Anti-Beggary Laws[118]

S. No.	States/Union Territories	Legislation in Force
	States	
1.	Andhra Pradesh	The Andhra Pradesh Prevention of Beggary Act, 1977
2.	Assam	The Assam Prevention of Begging Act, 1964
3.	Bihar	The Bihar Prevention of Begging Act, 1951
4.	Chhattisgarh	Adopted the Madhya Pradesh Bikshavirty Nivaran Adhiniyam, 1973
5.	Goa	The Goa, Daman & Diu Prevention of Begging Act, 1972
6.	Gujarat	Adopted the Bombay Prevention of Begging Act, 1959
7.	Haryana	The Haryana Prevention of Begging Act, 1971
8.	Himachal Pradesh	The Himachal Pradesh Prevention of Begging Act, 1979
9.	J&K	The J&K Prevention of Beggary Act, 1960
10.	Jharkhand	Adopted the Bihar Prevention of Begging Act, 1951
11.	Karnataka	The Karnataka Prevention of Begging Act, 1975
12.	Kerala	The Madras Prevention of Begging Act, 1945; the Trivancore Prevention of Begging Act, 1120; and the Cochin Vagrancy Act, 1120 are in force in different areas of the State.
13.	Madhya Pradesh	The Madhya Pradesh Bikshavirty Nivaran Adhiniyam, 1973
14.	Maharashtra	The Bombay Prevention of Begging Act, 1959
15.	Punjab	The Punjab Prevention of Begging Act, 1971
16.	Sikkim	The Sikkim Prohibition of Beggary Act, 2004
17.	Tamil Nadu	The Madras Prevention of Begging Act, 1945
18.	Uttar Pradesh	The Uttar Pradesh Prohibition of Begging Act, 1972

19.	Uttarakhand	Adopted the Uttar Pradesh Prohibition of Begging Act, 1972
20.	West Bengal	The West Bengal Vagrancy Act, 1943
	Union Territories	
21.	Daman & Diu	The Goa, Daman & Diu Prevention of Begging Act, 1972
22.	Delhi	Adopted the Bombay Prevention of Begging Act, 1959

Source: Press Information Bureau, Ministry of Social Justice & Empowerment, Government of India

The provisions of BPBA are also adopted by Jammu and Kashmir. Based on BPBA, 1959, the Jammu and Kashmir government enacted its own anti-begging law titled as "The Jammu and Kashmir, Prevention of Beggary Act, 1960"[119] in which definition of begging as well as the punishment for convicted are similar. Thus, for the purpose of discussing anti-begging laws in India, it is more suitable to discuss the BPBA, 1959.

Administration Critical Appraisal of Anti-Begging Laws

Begging is criminalized in cities such as Mumbai and Delhi as per the Bombay Prevention of Begging Act, BPBA (1959). Under this law, officials of the Social Welfare Department assisted by the police, conduct raids to pick up beggars who they then try in special courts called 'beggar courts'. If convicted, they are sent to certified institutions called 'beggar homes' also known as *'Sewa Kutir'* for a period ranging from one to ten years for detention, training and employment. The government of Delhi, besides criminalizing alms-seeking has also criminalized alms-giving on traffic signals to reduce the 'nuisance' of begging and ensure the smooth flow of traffic. According to B.B. Pande (1986)[120] the administration of beggary prevention laws may be examined at two levels:

(a)   the initial legal stage which encompasses arrest and pre-trial detention, and trial and sentencing; and

(b)   the administrative stage which involves detention, training and rehabilitation.

Pande (1986)[121] further described certain critical areas of legal administration in the context of the Union Territory of Delhi.

The Arrest

The Act has widely defined the offence of begging and it includes within its ambit not merely the actual soliciting for alms, but other acts directed towards that end, such as entering any private premises for the purposes of begging (section 2(1) (c)); or wandering about or remaining in a public place without visible means of subsistence (section 2(1) (d)); or allowing oneself to be used as an exhibit for soliciting alms (section 2(1) (e)). Section 2(1) (d) raises a sweeping presumption that the "singing," "dancing", "fortune telling", "performing", "putting any article for sale" of the offender is merely a pretence for receiving alms or begging. This section of the Act confers Powers on the police, social welfare officials and the courts to perceive one as beggar or not. Flawed perception of the objectives of this law, and the general bias of the system against the powerless and the weak, further contribute to the possibilities of misuse of power.

The lawful exercise of the powers of arrest remained become controversial. A study on the enforcement of the beggary law in Delhi has summed up the process of arrest thus:

The normal routine of the anti-beggary squad is to go out every morning to places like the vicinity of the railway stations, the inter-state bus terminus, temples and mosques. The squad usually consists of two men constables, two women constables and two or three of their henchmen who are long-term residents of a certified Institution. They seize such persons as they think are beggars - not many are caught while actually soliciting alms - and push them into the van and then move on for the next quarry. If the victim asks why he has been seized or where he is being taken or struggles against being put into the van, the captors' lathi comes down heavily on him. (Rao, 1980)[122]

Thus, the anti-begging squad may indiscriminately arrest the old and the young, the deplorable and the healthy, the faithless and the faithful. Often the members of distinct, self-employed professional groups like *saperas* (snake charmers), *kirtanias* (religious singers), *kanmailias* (ear cleaners), *nats* (acrobats and trapeze performers), *bazigars* (street magicians) and *jyotishis* (palmists) were also arrested by the raiding squad. (Rao 1981)[123]

The Trial

Persons picked up by anti-begging squad for the offence of beggary are tried by the Beggars' Court constituted in terms of the Act. The trial takes the form of a summary enquiry (the procedure prescribed in the Code of Criminal Procedure for the trial of summons cases is followed). According to Pande (1986) a large majority of the offenders lack resources for hiring a lawyer. For the unrepresented lot, the summary trial and its verdict is usually totally one-sided and alien. On the day of the trial, the alleged beggars are assembled before the courtroom well before the arrival of the magistrate. After the magistrate is through with other routine and administrative matters, the alleged beggars are ushered in one by one into the courtroom. A public prosecutor presents the case on behalf of the prosecution and only rarely, where the beggar is resourceful enough to afford a lawyer, there is a defence counsel. Usually the cases without a defence counsel of the uncontested cases are disposed of in less than two minutes - that is all the time the magistrate spares for 'examining' the charge papers, receiving the prosecution accusation and 'hearing' the beggar.

Generally, all those (arrested), who fail to give a satisfactory account of their employment, their presence in the town and all those who look ill, abandoned, or derelict are taken for beggars. The usual pattern of sentence, in the case of a person labelled a beggar, is either release on a bond ranging from ` 1000 to ` 2000 and a pledge not to beg in the future, or detention in a certified institution or the Beggar's Home or the Poor House for a period from one year to two years. A year's detention in the case of a person whose earnings in the town sustained his family, particularly those residing in the rural areas, would mean deprivation of one year's earnings, which could invariably have disastrous effects on the members of an entire family. (Pande 1986)[124]

Detention and Training

The post-sentence detention in the Beggar's Home is said to serve two objectives, namely, punishing and rehabilitating the beggar through treatment and training. In view of the growing emphasis on the rehabilitative ideal, the state beggary laws and the rules framed under according to high priority to the objective of training in various trades such as agriculture, gardening, weaving, tailoring, washing and dry cleaning, printing, and baking. However, the studies on the working of Beggar's Homes indicate a very low rate of success. According to the National Institute of Social Defence study, a very small percentage derive any benefit from training and other rehabilitative programmes meant for the inmates. The study observes in this context: *Only 42 per cent of the beggar population were imparted vocational training in the institution with a view to rehabilitating them, but recidivism was found high even in this segment. The attitudes of the inmates towards the institution was not constructive as 42 per cent of the inmates felt that the objective of sending them to the institution was to punish them.* (Pande 1986)[125]

Apart from the failures on the rehabilitation front the Beggar's Homes have of late become known for gross mismanagement and degrading physical conditions. The inmates were "treated like animals" inside these homes.

Finally, the existing institutional facilities for beggars and vagrants, even the ill-managed ones, are woefully inadequate for coping with the problem. The state beggary institution statistics reveal that for coping with the estimated national beggar population of 15 lakhs there are only 109 beggar institutes with inmate capacity of only 16,350. This means that the existing institutional facilities can be availed of by only 1.09 per cent of the beggar and vagrant population. Thus, in view of the poor impact of training and the limited institutional facilities, it can be surmised that in the existing scheme of things reform and rehabilitation of beggars and vagrants is a far cry. (Pande 1986)[126]

AAA and People's Union of Civil Liberties, PUCL have critiqued this Act and advocated for its repeal. Section 2(1) of the BPBA broadly defines 'beggars' as those individuals who directly solicit alms as well as those who have no visible means of subsistence and are found wandering around as beggars. Therefore, during the implementation of this law the homeless are often mistaken as beggars. Beggar homes, which are meant to provide vocational training, have been often found to have abysmal living conditions.

PROBLEMS FACED BY BEGGARS IN BEGGING LIFE

On question of problems faced by beggars, one beggar remarked *"Bheek mangna apne aap mein ek bahut badi problem hai. Is se zyada humein kya problem ho sakti hai humein!"* [Begging in itself is a major problem, what else more problems we can have!]. However, some problems faced by people in begging life in Jammu are enlisted as follows:

- People in begging usually lack a basic home along with basic facilities in that, although the concept of home and homelessness are subjective and may have different meanings for different people. They mostly live in *jhuggis*, or have no home and may sleep rough.

- They are socially excluded from the larger society and its various institutions.

- Some beggars face alienation and social isolation as they are not supported by family and relatives.

- Government is not bothered to help these beggars genuinely as there is no welfare scheme by government for the benefits of these unfortunate beggars.

- They are not treated as citizens by government as well as the society and many times face what Lankenau (1999)[127] termed as 'non-person treatment' by people.

- Beggars sometimes face harassment from locals for causing nuisance.

- In begging they also have to face threats from fellow beggars (competition over choosing place of begging etc.) as Dean (1999)[128] also argued that as a means of subsistence, it would seem, begging is a potentially hazardous activity situated within highly competitive and predatory social relations.

Health and hygienic problem

In beggar's perspective (and also in somewhat people's expectation) remaining dirty and unhygienic is prerequisite of begging. It is observed that they wear torn/dirty clothes as it make him look more needy and deserving of generosity of passer-by. Remaining dirty and eating unhygienic food is common among majority of beggars which makes them vulnerable for many diseases. In many ways, however, it was surprising that so many of the participants, in spite of their life-styles, stayed as fit as they appeared to be. Though, many beggars face health problems from simple to more severe one they hardly go for any medical consultation. Dean and Melrose (1999)[129] also found same found similar cases in their study. Almost half of their sample (nine participants) reported or claimed to have had health problems. In the worst such case, the participant would not seek medical help because there was an arrest warrant out for him and he was being sought by the police, although he fully expected that he would die from liver failure within a year or so. They further found that most of the beggars did not go hungry, but inevitably, some of them were not obtaining a satisfactory diet:

"I don't really eat healthy food or owt like that, you know what I mean. It's mostly junk food. I do get enough though. I reckon I do ... but some days, some days I'll just like, I just won't feel like eating at all, you know what I mean. I'll go a whole day without eating, but the next day I'll make up for it like."

Thus, it may be concluded that beggars came into begging due to various reasons which forced them to do so and due to their low background. They are the victims of social exclusion with deep rooted poverty. However, the state, firstly, is not interested in beggary issue and when it was pressurised by people it made an anti-beggary and anti-poor law which criminalises begging activity. Secondly, it is not interested in implementing this law as doing so may use a lot of its resources, thus, leaving begging issue in oblivion. The chapter, therefore, has helped in understanding (by discussion on) various reasons of begging in Jammu as well as in other states (through secondary literature).

NOTES

77 David Shichor, and Ruth Ellis. 1981. "Begging in Israel: An exploratory study." *Deviant Behavior* 2 (2): 109-125. doi:10.1080/01639625.1981.9967546.

78 Becker, Howard Saul. 1963. *Outsiders: Studies in the Sociology of Deviance*. New York: The Free Press.

79 UNDP. "Millennium Development Goals Indicators." *The official United Nations site for the MDG Indicators*. Accessed August 21, 2015. http://mdgs.un.org/unsd/mdg/Metadata.aspx?IndicatorId=0&SeriesId=597.

80 Op. cit. Ref. 1.

81 B.B Pande. 1986. "Rights of Beggars and Vagrants." *India International Centre Quarterly* 13 (4): 115-132. Accessed October 16, 2015. http://www.jstor.org/stable/23001440.

82 Nels Anderson. 1961. *The Hobo: The sociology of the homeless man*. The University of Chicago: Phoenix Books.

83 Tara Patel. 1959. "Some Reflections of the Beggar Problem in Ahmedabad." *Sociological Bulletin* 8 (1): 5-15. Accessed September 30, 2015. http://www.jstor.org/stable/42864545.

84 *"Poverty." merriam-webster. Accessed June 18, 2016. http://www.merriam-webster.com/dictionary/poverty.*

85 Alison Murdoch, Liz Connell, Jean Davis, and Joanne Maher. 1994. *We are human too: a study of people who beg*. London: Crisis.

86 2013. "Global employment trends 2013." *International Labour Organization*. January 21. Accessed December 29, 2015. (http://www.ilo.org/wcmsp5/groups/public/---dgreports/---dcomm/---publ/documents/publication/wcms_202326.pdf.

87 Karl Marx. 1863. *Capital: Theories of Surplus Value*. Vol. IV. Moscow: Progress Publishers. Accessed October 29, 2014. https://www.marxists.org/archive/marx/works/1863/theories-surplus-value/.

88 Op. cit. Ref. 9.

89 *UNESCO. 2004. The Plurality of Literacy and its implications for Policies and Programs. Position Paper, Paris: United Nations Educational, Scientific and Cultural Organization. Accessed January 13, 2016. http://unesdoc.unesco.org/images/0013/001362/136246e.pdf.*

90 Ibid.

91 WHO. n.d. "Disabilities." *World Health Organization*. Accessed May 17, 2016.

http://www.who.int/topics/disabilities/en/.

92 Op. cit. Ref. 9.

93 Christopher R. Stones. 2013. "A psycho-social exploration of street begging: A qualitative study." *South African Journal of Psychology* 43 (2): 157-166. doi:10.1177/0081246313482632.

94 *The Times of India.* 2016. "A dream shattered: Cops find starlet begging and stealing." April 26. Accessed November 4, 2015. http://timesofindia.indiatimes.com/city/mumbai/A-dream-shattered-Cops-find-starlet-begging-and-stealing/articleshow/51988079.cms.

95 *The Times of India.* 2007. "Gita's story: From ramp model to beggar." September 4. Accessed November 4, 2015. http://timesofindia.indiatimes.com/india/Gitas-story-From-ramp-model-to-beggar/articleshow/2335845.cms.

96 Op. cit. Ref. 9.

97 Ibid.

98 Jane Mathieson, Jennie Popay, Etheline Enoch, Sarah Escorel, Mario Hernandez, Heidi Johnston, and Laetitia Rispe. 2008. *Social Exclusion: Meaning, measurement and experience and links to health inequalities - A review of literature.* Background Paper, WHO. Accessed June 9, 2016.

99 Mack, Joanna. 2016. "Social exclusion." *Poverty.* January 21. Accessed June 2016, 17. http://www.poverty.ac.uk/definitions-poverty/social-exclusion.

100 International Encyclopedia of the Social Sciences. 2008. "Culture of Poverty." *Encyclopedia.com.* Accessed May 6, 206. http://www.encyclopedia.com/social-sciences/applied-and-social-sciences-magazines/culture-poverty.

101 Oscar Lewis. 1959. *Five Families: Mexican Case Studies in the Culture of Poverty.* New York: Basic Books.

102 Oscar Lewis. 1998. "The Culture of Poverty." *Society* 35 (2): 7-30. doi:10.1007/BF02838122.

103 Op. cit. Ref. 17.

104 Sonia Malik, and Sanjoy Roy. 2012. "A Study on Begging: A Social Stigma-An Indian Perspective." *Journal of Human Values* 18 (2): 187-199. doi:10.1177/0971685812454486.

105 Op. cit. Ref. 7.

106 NSID. 2014. "Beggary Prevention." *National Institute of Social Defence.* Accessed June 16, 2016.
http://www.nisd.gov.in/content/213_3_BeggaryPrevention.aspx.

107 Dennis J Baker. 2009. "A Critical Evaluation of the Historical and Contemporary Justifications for Criminalising Begging." *The Journal of Criminal Law* 48 (1): 212-240. doi:10.1177/0042098009360688.

108 Wikipedia Contributors. "Vagrancy (people)." *Wikipedia, The Free Encyclopedia.* Accessed March 16, 2016.
https://en.wikipedia.org/w/index.php?title=Vagrancy_(people)&oldid=741149179.

109 Ibid.

110 Dyutimoy Mukherjee. 2008. "Laws For Beggars, Justice for Whom: A Critical Review of the Bombay Prevention of Begging Act 1959." *The International Journal of Human Rights* 12 (2): 279-288. doi:10.1080/13642980801899709.

111 Op. cit. Ref. 5.

112 The Punjab Municipalities Act, 1911, the U.P. Municipalities Act, 1916, the C.P. and Berar Municipalities Act, 1922, etc.

113 The Madras City Police Act, 1833, the Calcutta Suburban Police Act, 1866 and the Bombay Police Act, 1861.

114 The Howrab Nuisance Act, 1866.

115 Op. cit. Ref. 5.

116 Hartley Dean, ed. 1999. *Begging Questions: Street-level economic activity and social policy failure.* Bristol: The Policy Press.

117 Op. cit. Ref. 31.

118 Ministry of Social Justice & Empowerment, GOI. 2016. *Press Information Bureau.* Accessed June 11, 2016.
http://pib.nic.in/newsite/PrintR.elease.aspx?relid=67734.

119 The Jammu and Kashmir, Prevention of Beggary Act, 1960

120 Op. cit. Ref. 5.

121 Ibid.

122 Amiya Rao, Sunil Battacharya, and Aurobindo Ghose. *A Report on Begging in Delhi.* PUCL.

[123] Amiya Rao. 1981. "Poverty and Power: The Anti-Begging Act." *Economic and Political Weekly* 16 (8): 269-270. Accessed February 02, 2016. http://www.jstor.org/stable/4369560.

[124] Op. cit. Ref. 5.

[125] Ibid.

[126] Ibid.

[127] Stephen E Lankenau. 1999. "Panhandling repertoires and routines for overcoming the nonperson treatment." *Deviant Behaviour* 20 (2): 183-206. doi:10.1080/016396299266551.

[128] Op. cit. Ref. 40.

[129] Hartley Dean, and Margaret Melrose. 1999. "Easy pickings or hard profession? Begging as an economic activity." In *Begging Questions: Street-level economic activity and social policy failure*, edited by Hartley Dean, 83-100. Bristol: The Policy Press.

4: BEGGARS AND SOCIETY: ENCOUNTERS AND TECHNIQUES

मांगन मरण समान है । मत मांगो कभी भीक ।
(*maangan maran samaan hai, mat maango kabhi bheek*)
मांगन से तो मारिवे भला । यह है सतगुरू की सीख ।
(*maangan se toh mariwey bhala, yeh hai satguru ki seekh*)
[*Begging is akin to dying, do not ask for alms. It's better to die than to beg, this is Satguru's advice (teaching).*] – Kabir

Begging is one of the oldest way to sustain oneself, prevalent among the poorest people in society. Throughout history the issue of beggars has raised discussion about utmost need, poverty, vagrancy and criminality. The present chapter has discussed and dealt with the encounters and interactions between beggars and the society, which includes: religious traditions of almsgiving, society's views on beggars, their reasons to give money to beggars, techniques used by beggars for soliciting alms, and social exclusion and stigma faced by the beggars.

Begging activity could not be understood in isolation, as an individual problem, but as a pattern of repetitive interactions between a beggar and society. Gore (1958)[130] is of the view that in earlier studies on the beggar 'problem' the focus of analysis has been the beggar himself, his mind, his attitudes, his handicap, his satisfaction, dissatisfaction, etc. He argued that such a mode of analysis is fallacious and misleading. It is fallacious because it loses sight of the fact that begging as a pattern of behaviour cannot be understood except as a process of interaction between the beggar and Society (giver). The begging activity is fundamentally based on the acquiescence of the members of the larger society. Begging as a repetitive pattern of behaviour, can only be understood as a process of interaction between two more or less institutionalized roles, that of the beggar and the giver. The beggar expresses a 'need' by stretching his hands in front of giver, toward which the giver's action is oriented. The giver meets this 'need' (of a beggar) by dropping a coin in the outstretched hand of the beggar: in meeting the need of the beggar in this particular way he is acting in accordance with certain 'norms' characteristic of his group and is simultaneously re-enforcing the beggar's particular pattern of meeting his need.

People's attitudes on begging differs considering its different aspects. As Gore (1958)[131] tried to explain begging activity as a whole consists of three interrelated aspects or acts of: Begging, Giving and Receiving and attitude of society to each of them varies greatly. This difference in attitude towards different aspects of begging is so not only in India, but throughout the world. Giving is encouraged, and begging is discouraged. Yet if there were no begging, there would be no need for giving - at least in the present restricted sense where giving is by definition oriented to the needs of a particular person and not to the impersonal needs of an institution. Further, there is a difference of attitude of society towards a beggar and a religious mendicant. Beggars may gain one's sympathy but not one's respect. However, mendicants (religious beggars) are still respected in Indian society, though it is too declining gradually. Begging is seen as a misfortune and a stigmatised activity. No person would have been begging unless he had to. But then - in the context of the Karma philosophy - no person can disclaim total responsibility even for his misfortunes. And, therefore, there is a sense of shame (stigma) attached to begging. The beggar experiences a loss of social status, even if his begging is due to factors entirely beyond his control.

WHY BEGGING OFFENDS?

Before discussing the other themes of this chapter, it is important to highlight why begging offends the other members of society. Erskine & McIntosh (1999)[132] are of the view that there are two particular aspects of begging which make it disliked by society: that those who beg may not be what they seem (*Frauds*), and questions about the amount of money that they make (*Income*). In other words, there is a general belief among people that those who beg, misrepresent themselves. They are not what they seem to be, they beg for their addiction (alcohol or even drugs) and not for a livelihood. They are fraud people associated with some gangs and may be involved in criminal activities. Moreover, many people believed that these beggars earn much more than a hardworking labourer. A few views (from present study) of people in this regard.

"In India begging became a profession and some more notorious criminals are involved in it."

"I don't give money to beggars, but when I pass homeless people I'm quite confused. I know, not all of them are cheaters but how to recognize it?"

"I suppose that all money is spent on cigarettes or alcohol (by beggars). *What is the most irritating thing is when you propose to buy something to eat and they don't want* (it)."

People, who are earning their livelihood through some kind of productive work do not like beggars' ways of living and also the way they earn money without doing any work. As Erskine & McIntosh (1999)[133] argues that it is the image of the 'merry life' which is one of the reasons that begging offends. This image depicts beggars as, at best 'wealthy cheats', and at least 'free from the constraints of society'. There is almost an element of jealousy here. They are seen as part of an alternative closed social group who speak a secret language and live in colonies, separate from rest of the society. General public have an impression of them as alcoholics, drug addicts and sexually immoral. Above all they may be dangerous, aggressive and criminals. Furthermore, 'Begging Encounter' too is awkward for the donor, because it involves making a moral judgement. Making such a judgement in a public place and promptly is difficult because it involves either the acceptance of the proffered interpretation of the encounter or the construction of an alternative one. This encounter is also problematic for the beggar also because, while at the same time as he or she creates the encounter, it also involves presenting him or herself as helpless and powerless.

RELIGION, ALMS-GIVING AND BEGGING

Begging is looked down upon in a social system, economic system as well as culture of a society. It is only religion which in one way or other (directly and indirectly), offers some support to begging by general emphasis on almsgiving. Alms or almsgiving involves giving to others as an act of virtue, either materially or in the sense of providing capabilities (e.g. education) for free[134]. It exists in a number of religions and regions. Following is a brief discussion on alms giving/charity in different religions.

Hinduism

'*Dana*' (in Hindi) or Charity is an ancient concept of almsgiving dating to the Vedic period of Hinduism. There are many types of *Dana* or alms in Hinduism but alms given to mendicants and beggars was known as *Bhiksha* in Vedic literature. The Rigveda has the earliest discussion of *Dana* in the Vedas and offers reasons for the virtue of alms-giving. The early Upanishads also discuss the virtue of almsgiving. '*Brihadaranyaka Upanishad*', for example, states that the three characteristics of a good, developed person are - self-restraint (*Damah*), compassion or love for all sentient life (*Daya*), and charity (*Dana*). Some scriptures, like the *Bhagavata Purana*, discusses when *Dana* is proper and when it is improper. It is stated that charity is inappropriate if it endangers and cripples modest livelihood of one's biological dependents or of one's own. Charity from surplus income above that required for modest living is recommended in the *Puranas*.[135]

Dana has been defined in traditional texts as any action of relinquishing the ownership of what one considered or identified as one's own, and investing the same in a recipient without expecting anything in return. '*Bhagvad Gita*[136]' discusses different modes of proper and improper charity or almsgiving

17.20 *"A gift is pure when it is given from the heart to the right person at the right time and at the right place, and when we expect nothing in return"*

17.21 *"But when it is given expecting something in return, or for the sake of a future reward, or when it is given unwillingly, the gift is a Rajas, impure."*

17.22 *"And a gift given to the wrong person at the wrong time and the wrong place, or a gift which comes not from the heart, and is given with proud contempt, is a gift of darkness."*

Giving *Dana* (charity) is considered as a very noble deed in Hinduism, to be (and should be) done without expectation of anything in return from the receiver of the charity. It is believed that charity is a form of good *Karma* that affects one's future circumstances and leads to good future life of the giver. However, many texts do not recommend charity to unworthy recipients or where charity may harm or encourage injury to or by the recipient. In Hinduism it is believed that charity is most effective when it is done with delight, a sense of "unquestioning hospitality", where the *Dana* ignores the short term weaknesses as well as the circumstances of the recipient and takes a long term view. From earlier times, Hindu temples have served as institutions for almsgiving as well as for getting alms.[137]

There are diverse types of *Danas* in various Hindu scriptures. Some of them are *Gau Dana* (donation of a cow), *Bhu Dana* (donation of land), and *Vidya Dana* (gift of knowledge and skills), *Aushadha Dana* (Charity of care for the sick and diseased), and *Anna Dana* (Giving food to the needy and all visitors) etc. Various Hindu texts suggest that among all these type of *Danas*, the *Vidya Dana* or the gift of knowledge is supreme *Dana*.[138]

Islam

In Islam, the concept of charity or almsgiving is generally divided into voluntary giving, i.e., *'Sadaqah'* and the *'Zakat'*, an obligatory practice of charity governed by a specific set of rules within Islamic jurisprudence. *Zakat* is the one of the five pillars of Islam. Various rules attached to the practice of *Zakat* but, in general terms, it is obligatory to give 2.5% of one's savings and business revenue and 5–10% of one's harvest to the poor. Like Hinduism, in Islam it is believed that all things belong to God and, therefore, wealth is held by human beings as trustees. A pious person may also give as much as he or she pleases as *Sadaqah*, and does so preferably in secret. According to *Shariah* charity is an act of worship. Ones possessions are purified by setting aside a proportion out of it for those in need.[139] Possible recipients of charity

(*Zakat* and *Sadaqah*) may include the extreme poor (destitute), the working poor, those who are unable to pay off their own debts, stranded travellers and others who need assistance, with the general principle of *Zakaah* always being that the rich should pay it to the poor (Benthall 1999)[140].

Muslims with wealth below a certain fixed threshold (*nisab*) do not have to pay *zakat* (Benthall 1999)[141]. According to Jonsson, (2006)[142] *Zakat* is obligatory (as per quran) when a certain amount of money, called the '*Nisab*', is reached or exceeded. The Nisab (or minimum amount) of gold and golden currency is 20 mithqal, approximately 85 grams of pure gold. One mithqal is approximately 4.25 grams. The nisab of silver and silver currency is 200 dirhams, which is approximately 595 grams of pure silver. The nisab of other kinds of money and currency is to be scaled to that of gold; the nisab of money is equivalent to the price of 85 grams of 999 type (pure) gold, on the day in which Zakat is paid.

Concept of alms-giving and charity in Islam, although, mainly stresses on sharing economic gains and considered economic prayer but it has much wider meaning as highlighted in following paragraph:

The Prophet said: 'Charity is a necessity for every Muslim.' He was asked: 'What if a person has nothing?' The Prophet replied: 'He should work with his own hands for his benefit and then give something out of such earnings in charity.' The Companions asked: 'What if he is not able to work?' The Prophet said: 'He should help poor and needy persons.' The Companions further asked 'What if he cannot do even that?' The Prophet said 'He should urge others to do good.' The Companions said 'What if he lacks that also?' The Prophet said 'He should check himself from doing evil. That is also charity.' (Charity: Islamic Center of Cedar Rapids)[143]

Buddhism

In Buddhism, alms or almsgiving is the respect given by a common Buddhist to a Buddhist monk, nun, spiritually developed person or another sentient being who is seeking alms. It is not charity as presumed by Western interpreters but it closely related to the concept of *Dana* in Hinduism. It is closer to a symbolic connection to the spiritual realm and to show humbleness and respect in the presence of the secular society. The act of alms giving assists in connecting the human to the monk or nun and what he/she represents. As the Buddha has stated:

Householders & the homeless or charity [monastics] in mutual dependence both reach the true Dhamma....[144]

In Buddhism, "almsgiving" and, more generally, "giving" are called *"Dana"*. Such giving is one of the three elements of the path of Dhamma (practice) as formulated by the Buddha for laypeople. This path of practice for laypeople is: *dana, sila, bhavana*. There is a general belief in Buddhism that the more a person gives – and the more one gives without seeking something in return – the wealthier (in the broadest sense) one will become. By giving one destroys those acquisitive impulses that ultimately lead to further suffering. Generosity is also expressed towards other sentient beings as both a cause for merit and to aid the receiver of the gift. Generosity towards other sentient beings is greatly emphasised in Mahayana tradition of Buddhism.[145] In Buddhism, giving of alms is the starting point of one's journey to *Nirvana*. In practice, one can give anything with or without thought for *Nirvana*. (Dharma Data: Nirvana)[146]

Christianity

In Christianity, the almsgiving is an act of charity toward the less fortunate and destitute. From the Apostolic age, in Christianity, giving alms was considered an expression of love which was first expressed by God to them, as when Jesus Christ sacrificed himself as an act of love for the salvation of believers. The offertory is the traditional moment practiced in Christianity (especially among Catholics) when alms were collected. Some Protestant groups, such as Baptists and Methodists, also engage in giving alms, although it is more commonly referred to as "tithes and offerings" by the church. Some Christian fellowships practice regular giving for special purposes called 'Love Offerings' for the poor, destitute or victims of disastrous loss such as home fires or medical expenses. In Orthodox theology, almsgiving is considered an important part of the spiritual life. The Bible put emphasis on giving out of love and not out of duty as illustrated below.[147]

"I tell you the truth, whatever you did, not do for one of the least of these, you did not do for me." – [Matthew 25:45][148]

In the majority of Christian forms of worship and denominations, a collection of "tithes and offerings" is given for the support of the church's mission, budget, ministry, and for its relief of the poor, as an important act of Christian charity, united to communal prayer. In some churches the "offering plate" or "offering basket" is placed upon the altar, as a sign that the offering is made to God, and a sign of the bond of Christian love. In addition, private acts of charity, considered virtuous only if not done for others to admire, are seen as a Christian duty.[149]

Thus, from this discussion on almsgiving tradition in some of the prominent religions of the world as well as of India, it can be noted that all religions put great emphasis on almsgiving. Charity or almsgiving is prescribed for all individuals who are capable of doing towards the benefits of fellow beings who are destitute and are unable to earn by themselves due to various reasons. Another point which is emphasised is that an individual should donate or give without expecting anything in return, although, he may be spiritually enriched. Some major religions of India like Hinduism and Buddhism even championed a life of renunciation, detached from the material world, and living on alms (Bhiksha) solicited from others. Thus, these Indian religions not only have almsgiving traditions but also the alms-soliciting traditions like that of *Sadhus, Sanyasis, Fakirs, Bhikshuks* etc. This makes begging in India more extensive than other countries of the world.

TECHNIQUES USED FOR SOLICITING ALMS BY BEGGARS

There are some studies which focused their attention on the techniques used by beggars while soliciting alms from public. Shichor and Ellis (1981)[150] in their study, found that there were several methods used by beggars on their jobs. They pointed out that some of them stood or sat quietly in public places and waited with extended hands or tin cups for passers-by to give them alms. Others pled, sometimes loudly, for charity. Some beggars approach pedestrians and demand money from them; if pedestrians refuse them, they may get cursed by beggars loudly. In addition, there are beggars who go from shop to shop asking for money. They do it on a regular basis and usually have a turf and establish a permanent relationship with the shops in their area. A few beggars play music on stringed instruments while asking for charity. They may apparently did not understand music at all but still try to make noise in an attempt to draw more public attention. Some of the beggars wore special "working clothes," which were torn and dirty to make the wearers look more needy. But there were others, mainly the older ones, who tried to keep themselves clean and tidy. They were also the quietest and the most embarrassed by their engagement in begging.

K.L. Kamat in his article *'The begging profession'*[151] argued that the beggars have to care about their attire just like actors and performers. People who beg in the name of the religion have to grow beard, wear saffron (*kavi*) clothes and ash etc. Others who pose as destitute have to dress up dirty and torn clothes which make them look vulnerable. The beggars have to master the art of begging just as they have to master the art of dressing up. They realize that it is very difficult to refuse a hungry man begging just as you come out of a popular restaurant. While a woman begs in the name of her husband who is in the death bed in a hospital, it is not uncommon that the husband is begging in his wife's name on the next street. A pregnant woman will say that her previous child has died, and she needs money for the funeral. Her heart-rendering appeal fetches good money, yet nobody knows if any of her six children has died. An entire family will beg by saying that they lost everything in the floods. The children and women in scanty clothing will be sleeping on the road side and the head of the household blocks the passers-by for small change. Thus, some major techniques used by beggars in Jammu can be discussed briefly as follows:

1. Sitting at a particular place: By sitting at a particular place and putting a bowl in front of them or a piece of cloth and some coins or paper notes (money) in it. Most of such beggars are either disabled or elderly but able-bodied beggars can also be seen using this technique especially in religious places. They may just sit and spread hand and not utter a word in solicitation of money; or they may seek for money by humble request. This request depends on the place and occasion. If they are begging in front of a temple they would just say *'Jai Mata Di'*, *'Jai Shree Ram'*, *'De do bhaiya/beta/beti bhagwan tumhara bhala karega'* etc.; in front of Muslim Shrine/mosques *'Allah tumhari har murad puri karega, de do'*. In this technique, they just try to receive attention of altruistic donors. This technique is helpful for the beggars as it causes not much nuisance to public, and those who do not want to give alms to beggars can move on without much moral dilemma.

2. Telling pitiable stories: Many beggars have some unfortunate tales about their misery but as the nature of their profession they brief it only in about one or two lines (however, if anyone further asks them they have full version of the story). Like '*Bete ke ilaj keliye paise chahiye, kuch madad kar do*' (need money for son's treatment, please help) or '*Kuch khaya ni hai do din se*' (didn't eat for last two days). This technique is mainly used by beggars who follow a migration or rotation pattern and who beg in highly crowded area or in residential areas (or colonies). Stories by beggars are conveyed symbolically through down-and-out facial expressions, as Ray (a beggar) narrates in a study by Lankenau (1999)[152]: *People look at me— the way I talk and you know—feel sorry for me. They know I'm homeless by the way I'm lookin'! And I give them a sad little look.* Same kind of tactics were observed and also acknowledged by some beggars in Jammu city too.

3. Irritating passer-by: Another technique for soliciting alms is by irritating passer-by, by continuously following them until they give money to these beggars. While doing so some may even get aggressive if the passer-by refuses them. They are most annoying type of beggars and are responsible for bringing bad name to beggar community.

4. Distributing appeal cards: beggars also use to solicit money by distributing small cards of appeal for begging, some beggars (mostly young girls in context of present study) carry appeal cards with them and use these for begging from people. After distributing cards, they utter these lines '*De do behn ji/bhaiya*' and sometime requests by touching the feet of people. The image 4.2 is an example of Appeal Cards used for begging.

5. Offering unwanted services: Some beggars (usually younger, comparatively) use the technique of offering unwanted services like cleaning glasses of vehicles, or selling flowers and then soliciting for money. They are mostly found at traffic signals. They too sometimes become aggressive when they get refused for alms.

Pity/Compassion as a Major Tool

During fieldwork, beggars were asked about their opinion as to why people give money to them? Most the beggars (handicapped, old and weak) responded that people gave alms to them because they may felt pity on their conditions and show sympathy towards them. While begging, a beggar has to play a role of a salesman (who have to sell 'Nothing'), a strategist and an artist. They know that people give money to them out of pity, so their main task is to present themselves as pitiable, weak and helpless. The more pitiable they present themselves in public the more alms they will get. For this most beggars wear torn and dirty clothes, don't bath (not even wash their hands and face) when they go out for begging.

Clothing, appearances, and presentation of self may also be manipulated or used to tell the desired story. In fact, becoming a successful storyteller is contingent on developing a look that works, as one beggar argued:

When I first started begging, I couldn't understand as to why people weren't giving me money – maybe I looked too neat clean. So, I grew this shabby beard and figured this trick of the profession. As long as I was looking presentable like I was doing a 9-to-5 job. Similar kinds of tools used by beggars were also found in Lankenau's (1999)[153] study.

Role of Disability and Gender in Getting Alms

Shichor & Ellis, (1981)[154] mentioned that physical handicaps are an important component of begging. For instance, the crippled and blind beggars of London displayed their handicaps while engaged in begging. Many beggars had some kind of handicap that they used in the process of begging. Similarly, Fabrega and Manning (1974) indicated the importance of physical handicaps in begging in Mexico. In this study, those who were handicaps usually claimed that they were "entitled" to receive charity. They displayed their handicaps and waited for the public to notice them and give them alms. Chandra (1967) claimed that 26 percent of the beggars surveyed in Lucknow, India, used the technique of "exhibiting physical handicaps and diseases both genuine and false."

Handicaps serve not only as a device for asking for charity but also as justification for engagement in begging. Some of those who did not have a physical handicap chose to turn to the public in a demanding tone to establish their claim.

People were asked that to which type of beggar they would prefer to give money if they had to? Most people responded that they would like to give it to the disable beggars as they could not earn by any other source. So disable beggars earn more than the able bodied one if both beg in same area but as able bodied can move from places to places they may earn enough. While no significant difference was found between earnings of male and female beggars.

Use of Religious Sentiments

For Shichor & Ellis, (1981)[155] an important factor in the "trade" (begging) is religious observance. It has been noted that the Jewish religion values charity highly. One of the beggars, in their study, who was not an observant Jew nonetheless wore a skullcap (worn by religious male Jews). He explained that he was only trying to cope with "professional reality, " because observant people are more inclined to give alms and prefer to give to observant beggars. Appeals to religious feelings in the process of begging is a universal practice.

In the present study, most beggars agreed that they use religious sentiments while begging from passer-by. They may simply use these type of phrases:

Jai Mata Ki, Jai Bhole Nath, Hari Om, Jai Shani Dev, Jai Shree Ram or
Bhagwan Ke Naam Pe De De, Bhagwan Tumhara bhala karega
Allah Ke Naam Pe De De, Allah Tumhari Har Murad Puri Kare Ga. [all equivalently means give me in the name of God] And So On…

As discussed in detail, begging is sanctioned by religion. Beggars take advantage of this and use religion as a tool in begging. During the study, it was also found that the beggars irrespective of their religion, were found begging at different religious places. For example, a few Muslims were found begging in front of *'Kali Mata'* temple in *Bawe* (a place in Jammu city). One said *"Allah keliye to hum sab brabar hain, Allah bhagwan ek hi to hai… Humein do waqt ki roti mil jaye bas itna hi chahiye."* [God is one, no matter what name we give him – Allah, Bhagwan etc. We all are equals in front of him. It would be enough for us if we get two-time meal daily].

Beggars also used different attires during different days to beg (as they considered this a technique to get more alms and earn more). In Hindu philosophy, there are different days which are meant for specific God and Goddess, beggars also catch up with the myth as they can be seen carrying a photograph of *Mata Durga* and *Lord Hanuman* on Tuesday, carrying idol of *Lord Shiva* on Monday and there are so many who go door to door especially on Saturday carrying an idol of '*Shani Dev*' to beg alms. Beggars also adopt the other religious or social ethos as required in a particular setting to make an emotional appeal to the passer by. But one of the limitation the researcher was not able to overcome was that the beggars who use this as a technique did not reveal their own religion.

UNDERSTANDING DONOR'S REASON FOR GIVING

The beggars carry different images in the eyes of common people. Pushkar Raj (2005)[156] argues that for some they are no more than beggars, while others treat them as anti-social elements. Looking at their clothes and the way they are forced to live, there would hardly be anyone who would think of them as similar to any other people trying to earn their livelihood. Though the reputation of beggars, in general is not good among people but still most people at some point of time give money or alms to these beggars. The theory of Ethnic Nepotism by Butovskaya (2000)[157] also hold some ground in context of the present study. According to this theory people are more likely to give money to the beggars belonging to their own ethnic groups (religious communities in Indian context) than to the beggars from outside of their etnic groups.

Hermer (1999)[158] is of the view that the impulse of the passers-by to give may be located in a number of feelings such as guilt, pity, embarrassment or resentment. But the important point is that the outcome of giving represents compassionate[§§] conduct and

---

[§§] Compassion is a feeling or emotion that moves someone to express pity or mercy, to relieve the suffering or stress of another.

instantaneous pity.

Here are a few views of people which may illustrate why people give to beggars even after disliking them.

"Jo handicap hai us pe taras aa jata hai aur dene ka man bi krta hai. Lekin jis ki do aankhen, do hath, do tange hoon wo khud bi kama sakta hai" [I feel pity for the handicaps and like to give money to them but those who have two eyes, two arms and two legs (means able-bodied person) they could (and should) earn for themselves (by some other work)]

"Subah subah un ki bad-dwa ni leni chahiye is liye de dete hain 5-10 rupaiye." [In early morning one should not be cursed by them (beggars), that is why (I) gave them 5-10 rupees]. - A Shopkeeper

"Kisi shubh kaam pe jaa rahe hoon ya achhe din ki umeed rakhni ho to maangne wale ko mana ni krna chahiye." [If one is going for some very important work or wish for a good day ahead then he should not refuse a beggar].

"Kabhi Kabhi acha mood hota hai to de deta hun ni toh kis kis ko dete rahenge." [Sometime when I am in good mood, I give (money to beggars) otherwise it is not possible to give as there so many (beggars)].

I have a soft heart for beggars. Sad to see people sitting on sidewalks asking for alms with nothing to eat. The government should work harder to lessen beggars in the street.

"Begging is like casteism, though, both are illegal but both are with us in open and government cannot do anything. Why? Because both are sanctioned by Religion!"

"The government should make a policy to helps them out for their problems. it really makes me sad how beggars numbers is increasingly fast."

The reasons cited by people in Jammu can be generalised into following:

o   Feeling of Guilt
o   Feel pity on poor and disabled
o   To get rid of them as they are annoying
o   Sometime depends on mood
o   Because others around them are also giving
o   Give in name of God
o   To help them as they are needy.

In India as well as in Jammu, there is a very strong feeling of Religiosity and superstition among people. Most of the people are guided by the religious idea of not disappointing a beggar at a house as well as at work.

HOW BEGGARS ARE TREATED BY PEOPLE?

As beggars are among the most vulnerable group, they may become easy targets for harassment at the hands of general public. Dean (1999)[159] found that a majority of the sample (in his study) had been subject to violence or assault while begging. Such incidents included systematic beatings by vigilantes, casual violence from passers-by (characteristically, young, male and drunk), and abusive behaviour (spitting, the throwing of cigarette ends, the kicking over of the participant's hat or board).

"I get attacked about once a week. Yeah, pushed or someone tries to kick you.... Only about once a week, it's not often, [but] sometimes as many as two or three times." "I suppose [name] would have got abuse – that's the girl I beg with, she'd have got abuse at least once a day anyway. At the weekends it was terrible, the abuse, 'cos they were all drunk and loud and jumping about. I don't know, they're revolting."

In Dean's (1999)[160] study two participants reported significant injuries from such attacks and another claimed he had known of beggars who had been killed. However, as several participants explained, violence, intimidation and theft could also be perpetrated on beggars by other beggars and street-people. Several participants expressed their sense of vulnerability and two explained how they had on occasions been approached by people who would demand that they hand over their session's takings. In Edinburgh, one participant described the practice as the 'taxing' of beggars. 'Taxing' has been observed – in the recent past, at least – to have been rife on the streets of London.

However, in present study, though some beggars have reported harassment few times, majority said they did not face much harassment. One beggars said that a few goons sometimes come to their *Jhuggis* and demand money from them, or else they (goons) will throw them in river Tawi.

Beggars (mostly able-bodied) sometimes face condemnation from general public that instead of engaging themselves in begging they should do some work. One instance as observed during fieldwork where a matador conductor condemning a female beggar: *"Sharam aani chahiye tum logon ko bheek maangte ho, bahar se aake yahan gand failate ho. Jaavo Kaam kro kuch."* [Shame on you people. You come from other states and pollute our state too. Go and do some other work].

Police usually do not take actions against beggars but sometimes as a cleanliness drive (or similar situation), they stop them from begging for a few days. A beggar narrates: *"Jab koi khas program hota hai to Police wale bhaga dete hain lekin dusre teesre din hum fir wapis aa jate hai kaam pe."* [Whenever there is some special programme, the police send us away but after two - three days we again come back to resume our work].

It is therefore signified that, among the beggars also, some are pitied by the society and some are cursed.

Begging and Social Exclusion: Stigma in begging

Social exclusion is a complex and multi-dimensional process. It involves the lack or denial of resources, rights, goods and services, and the inability to participate in the normal relationships and activities, available to the majority of people in a society, whether in economic, social, cultural or political arenas. It affects both the quality of life of individuals and the equity and cohesion of society as a whole. Amartya Sen (2000)[161] explains that the term "social exclusion" is of relatively recent origin first discussed in the writings of René Lenoir in 1974. The notion has, however, already made substantial inroads into the discussions and writings on poverty and deprivation. There is a large and rapidly growing literature on the subject. The concept of social exclusion is seen as covering a remarkably wide range of social and economic problems. Even in the practical context of identifying "the excluded" in France, René Lenoir, spoke of the following as constituting the "excluded" - a tenth - of the French population:

"mentally and physically handicapped, suicidal people, aged invalids, abused children, substance abusers, delinquents, single parents, multi-problem households, marginal, asocial persons, and other social 'misfits'".

The literature that has followed Lenoir's original initiative has vastly added to this already bulging list of the "socially excluded." As Silver (1995)[162] notes, the list of "a few of the things the literature says people may be excluded from" must include the following:

"a livelihood; secure, permanent employment; earnings; property, credit, or land; housing; minimal or prevailing consumption levels; education, skills, and cultural capital; the welfare state; citizenship and legal equality; democratic participation; public goods; the nation or the dominant race; family and sociability; humanity, respect, fulfilment and understanding".

Beggars have faced exclusion from the prevailing social system and its rights and privileges, typically as a result of poverty or the fact of belonging to a minority social group. They are not considered important in economy, culture and politics of the larger society of which they too are the members. As Dean (1999)[163] argued that begging is conducted beyond the norms of formal economic activity, and it is a socially excluded or excluding form of behaviour. Begging is, in economic terms, a marginalised activity, and also beggars are normatively excluded from the values, prejudices and aspirations of other citizens.

In few instances, in recent times, begging is used as an instrument of protest against the establishments or system (state or its agencies) to shame them. Begging activity was used (in few instances) for shaming the government by certain sections of the society, so that their voice may get heard. Following stories in a leading national newspaper tells the tale in much clear words.

Doctors take out march with begging bowls (Feb 3, 2016; The Times of India)[164]: "New Delhi: Almost 18,000 doctors and nurses working at North and East Corporation hospitals on Tuesday took out a march from the Civic Centre to Rajghat in protest against non-payment of salaries. Armed with stethoscopes, lab coats and begging bowls, the protesters were seen telling passer-by that CM Arvind Kejriwal and PM Narendra Modi had orphaned them and hence they were out on streets, asking for money."

Parents go 'begging' to protest steep school fees (Apr 5, 2016; The Times of India)[165]: "Ludhiana: Parents have found a novel way of opposing the hefty development charges being levied by private unaided schools every year. On Tuesday, parents of children studying in different schools begged for money at the Mini Secretariat, to pay for the development fund of schools. The parents are complaining against the high fee, commercial activities, and costly book sets."

Activist 'begs' to protest government's failure of school schemes (Jul 1, 2016; The Times of India)[166]: "Coimbatore: A social activist was on Thursday arrested for seeking alms in front of the district collectorate here to mark his protest against the state government's failure to distribute free school bags and shoes to government students."

All these incidents indicate that how begging is considered as a stigmatised activity and has been used by different sections to humiliate government. Hence, it can be concluded that begging is very low and stigmatised activity according to majority society perspective. For them begging means, degradation of a person or group to the lowest level with a loss of self-esteem and dignity.

NOTES

---

130 Madhav Sadashiv Gore. 1958. "Society and the Beggar." *Sociological Bulletin* 7 (1): 23-48. Accessed September 30, 2015. http://www.jstor.org/stable/42864528.

131 Ibid.

132 Angus Erskine, and Ian McIntosh. 1999. "Why begging offends: historical perspectives and continuities." In *Begging Questions: Street-level economic activity and social policy failure*, edited by Hartley Dean, 27-42. Bristol: The Policy Press

133 Ibid.

134 Wikipedia contributors. n.d. "Alms." *Wikipedia, The Free Encyclopedia*. Accessed June 14, 2016. https://en.wikipedia.org/wiki/Alms.

135 Ibid.

136 A.C. Bhaktivedanta Swami Prabhupada. 1983. *Bhagvad Gita - As it is*. California: Bhaktivedanta Book Trust International

137 Burton Stein. 1960. "The Economic Function of a Medieval South Indian Temple." *The Journal of Asian Studies* 19 (2): 163-76. doi:10.2307/2943547.

138 Op. cit. Ref. 5

139 Jonathan Benthall. 1999. "Financial Worship: The Quranic Injunction to Almsgiving." *The Journal of the Royal Anthropological Institute* 5 (1): 27-42. doi:10.2307/2660961.

140 Ibid.

141 Thierry Kochuyt. 2009. "God, Gifts and Poor People: On Charity in Islam." *Social Compass* 56 (1): 98–116. doi:10.1177/0037768608100345..

142 D. Jonsson. (2006). *Islamic Economics and the Final Jihad: The Muslim Brotherhood to the Leftist/Marxist - Islamist Alliance*. California: Xulon Press.

143 *Charity: Islamic Center of Cedar Rapids*. Retrieved June 12, 2016, from http://crmosque.com/islam-101/charity-zakah

144 *Dharma Data: Nirvana*. Retrieved August 11, 2016, from Buddhanet: http://www.buddhanet.net/e-learning/dharmadata/fdd43.htm

145 Ibid.

146 Romila Thapar. 1981. "The householder and the renouncer in the Brahmanical and Buddhist traditions." *Contributions to Indian Sociology* 15 (1): 273-298. doi:10.1177/006996678101500115.

147 Op. cit. Ref. 5.

148 Matthew (Bible) 25:45 (http://biblehub.com/matthew/25-45.htm)

149 Matthew (Bible) 5:23–24
(http://tools.wmflabs.org/bibleversefinder/?book=Matthew&verse=5:23–24&src=KJV)

150 David Shichor, and Ruth Ellis. 1981. "Begging in Israel: An exploratory study." *Deviant Behavior* 2 (2): 109-125. doi:10.1080/01639625.1981.9967546.

151 K.L. Kamat. 1997. "The Begging Profession." *Kamat's Potpourri*. August 15. Accessed May 24, 2016. http://www.kamat.com/kalranga/bhiksha/begging.htm

152 Stephen E Lankenau. 1999. "Panhandling repertoires and routines for overcoming the nonperson treatment." *Deviant Behaviour* 20 (2): 183-206. doi:10.1080/016396299266551.

153 Ibid.

154 Op. cit. Ref. 21.

155 Ibid.

156 Pushkar Raj. 2005. *Criminalising poverty: Houseless and anti-beggary law in Delhi.* New Delhi: PUCL Bulletin. Accessed January 30, 2016. http://www.pucl.org/Topics/Industries-envirn-resettlement/2004/criminalise-poverty.htm.

157 M. Butovskaya, F. Salter, I. Diakonov, and A. Smirnov. 2000. "Urban Begging and Ethnic Nepotism in Russia: An Ethological Pilot Study." *Human Nature* 11 (2): 157-182. doi:10.1007/s12110-000-1017-z.

158 Hermer, J. (1999). Policing Compassion: begging, law and power in public places. Ph.D. Thesis, University of Oxford.

159 Hartley Dean, and Margaret Melrose. 1999. "Easy pickings or hard profession? Begging as an economic activity." In *Begging Questions: Street-level economic activity and social policy failure*, edited by Hartley Dean, 83-100. Bristol: The Policy Press.

160 Ibid.

161 Sen, Amartya. 2000. *Social Exclusion: Concept, Application, and Scrutiny.* Manila: Asian Development Bank.

162 Ibid.

163 Hartley Dean, ed. 1999. *Begging Questions: Street-level economic activity and social policy failure.* Bristol: The Policy Press.

164 *The Times of India.* 2016. "Doctors take out march with begging bowls." February 3. Accessed March 4, 2016.
http://timesofindia.indiatimes.com/city/delhi/Doctors-take-out-march-with-begging-bowls/articleshow/50827751.cms.

165 *The Times of India.* 2016. "Parents go 'begging' to protest steep school fees." April 5. Accessed April 8, 2016.
http://timesofindia.indiatimes.com/city/ludhiana/Parents-go-begging-to-protest-steep-school-fees/articleshow/51705017.cms.

166 *The Times of India.* 2016. "Activist 'begs' to protest government's failure of school schemes." July 1. Accessed July 13, 2016.
http://timesofindia.indiatimes.com/city/coimbatore/Activist-begs-to-protest-govt-failure-of-school-schemes/articleshow/53001320.cms?from=mdr.

5 CONCLUSION

Begging is a form of street-level economic activity. Begging is the practice or an economic activity whereby a person obtains money, food or other things from people they encounter by request without the intention of returning. Begging is an ancient, widespread and enigmatic (controversial) occupation. Although varying by geography and the times, begging is universal. People who beg are among the most vulnerable in society, often trapped in poverty and deprivation, and it is regarded as a risky and demeaning activity. The present research study has explored the socio-cultural and economic life of the beggars (persons engaged in begging) in Jammu city. The study has looked into the deplorable conditions of the beggars in the city and has explored the reasons and causes of begging. The study also focused on the interaction process between the beggars and the society.

In India, poverty and unemployment are still serious issues to be addressed as these are the prime causes of a number of other social problems and issues of serious concern. Beggary is one such issue born out of the destitution and unemployment. Moreover, Begging is not a one-dimensional phenomenon/activity as already noted. In all its dimensions, begging, further have two opposite facets like, it has a *cultural-religious* aspect, in this aspect alms giving is encouraged by religious traditions on one hand but on the other hand these alms could be solicited by frauds or fake mendicants. It has a *social* aspect, in which begging is a social problem for society in general, but at the same time it is life saviour for people in extreme poverty, and acts as a relief from destitution for beggars. In *political* aspect, government is not addressing this issue of beggary and extreme poverty properly, although all democratic governments in India asserts that they work for the poor. And more importantly, *economic* aspect where begging acts as a livelihood for people on the edge/destitute while on the other hand beggars are seen as parasites and burden by larger society. In its every aspect begging represents a dualism between society and beggar.

Begging activity could not be understood in isolation as an individual problem but as a pattern of repetitive interactions between a beggar and society. Gore (1958), is of the view that in earlier studies on the beggar 'problem' the focus of analysis has been the beggar himself, his mind, his attitudes, his handicap, his satisfaction, dissatisfaction, etc. He argued that such a mode of analysis is fallacious and misleading. It is fallacious because it loses sight of the fact that begging as a pattern of behaviour cannot be understood except as a process of interaction between the beggar and the giver. Begging requires the acquiescence of the members of the larger society. As begging is a repetitive pattern of behaviour, it can be understood only as a process of interaction between two more or less institutionalized roles, that of the beggar and that of the giver. The beggar stretches out a hand and expresses a 'need' toward which the giver's action is oriented. The giver meets this 'need' by dropping a coin in the outstretched hand of the beggar: in meeting the need of the beggar in this particular way he is acting in accordance with certain 'norms' characteristic of his group and is simultaneously re-enforcing the beggar's particular pattern of meeting his need. He further tried to explain begging as consisting of three interrelated acts of Begging, Giving and Receiving and attitude of society to each of them varies greatly. This is so not only in our society, but in all societies. Giving is encouraged, and begging is discouraged. Yet if there were no begging, there would be no need for giving - at least in the present restricted sense where giving is by definition oriented to the needs of a particular person and not to the impersonal needs of an institution. Gore (1958), further argues that the attitude of society to a person who asks for alms, but is not a religious mendicant is different. As a beggar he claims one's sympathy but not one's respect. Begging itself is a misfortune. No person would beg unless he had to. But then-in the context of the Karma philosophy-no person can disclaim total responsibility even for his misfortunes. And, therefore, there is a sense of shame attached to begging. The beggar experiences a loss of social status, even if his begging is due to factors entirely beyond his control.

Begging activity is mainly of three types,

i) Passive begging – in which beggars either sit or stand at one spot with a sign alerting passers-by that they need money or an extended hand towards passers-by, without asking for money.

ii) *Active begging* is a type of begging in which beggars follow a passers-by and ask for money, but they easily hold back (or stop) when refused. They do not employ any forms of standover tactics.

iii) *Aggressive begging* techniques refer to obtaining money from members of the public by using stand-over tactics and threatening speech or behaviour. Aggressive techniques elicit fear and discomfort and often border on criminal assault. All these types of begging are observed in Jammu city too, although, the aggressive begging is less prevalent in Jammu.

There is a much diversity among beggar population. Different types of Beggars could be seen begging around. They can be classified into different categories.

On the basis of the need, beggars can be classified as *Genuine* and *Fraudulent* – Genuine beggar refers to an individual who is in dire need of money and who does not misrepresent himself in the course of soliciting donations. Typically, a genuine beggar is unable to engage in alternative economic activities, while a fraudulent beggar is an individual who, while economically downtrodden, intends to misrepresent himself in an effort to gain the benefits that an altruistic donor might be willing to bestow on a genuine beggar. Fraudulent beggar is also poor but he could be engaged in alternative economic activity and has Purposively chosen begging.

On the basis of their physical traits they can be classified as *Old* (elderly) beggars i.e., beggars above the age of 60 years; *Child* beggars i.e. beggars below the age of 14 years; *Disabled* beggars (includes physically handicapped like crippled, blind, deaf etc.); *Able-bodied* beggars i.e., those beggars who are young and seems fit and can be engaged in other works, and; religious *Mendicant* i.e., those beggars who choose begging as prescribed by their religion or sect. Old, disabled, able-bodied, and mendicant are included in the present research but child beggars were not a part of the present study.

On the basis of reason of begging, beggars can be classified into three categories: beggar by *Circumstances* i.e., those unfortunate individuals who are pushed into begging because of their circumstances like destitution, disruptive family etc.; beggar by *Culture*, there are various communities for whom begging is a hereditary occupation, so they are in begging because of their culture; beggar by *Habit*, there are few beggars who even though have family members to support them but still they like to beg as part of their habit (as previously they were in begging). There are some beggars who are so used to begging that they actually prefer not to work. Most beggars as described in the above typologies were also found in Jammu city.

The Begging activity is associated with various dilemmas - ethical, moral or others. Firstly, the dilemma is faced by beggars when choosing this activity as their job (as they view it) because begging is considered a stigmatised, deviant and illegal activity (in context of present study). Choosing such an activity is very risky (in social as well as in legal terms) for them. Again while begging they may also face the dilemma of whether to misrepresent (presenting themselves as helpless, *Bechara garib*) themselves or not and whether they should approach a particular person (as s/he may harass them or give them money) or not. As there is a paradox that if a person is genuinely poor he does not go out for asking money from people but (Gore 1958)[167], if he does so (as per paradox), how could the generous people (who are willing to donate) could find and help him. If one is actively soliciting for money, s/he may be seen as fraudulent.

The begging problem is also a dilemma for 'Welfare State' and its government - which is supposed to take care of the poorest, disadvantaged and needy - that whether it should suppress begging by taking strict action against beggars (if they do so they will be seen as autocratic state) or control it by providing them economic support (if they do so it will encourage idleness and parasitism and a lot of money is needed for their welfare). This may be the reason behind the silence of welfare states on 'Begging issue'. However, this is a kind of issue which government alone cannot tackle. It needs support of everyone.

Finally, 'begging encounter' also becomes a dilemma for Public or society, which claims that they should help the poor and needy fellows by giving alms (according to religious & spiritual traditions). They too are caught in dilemma when they encounter a beggar, and has to perceive from his/her attitude that whether s/he is actually needy or just a fraud, what will s/he do with their money (will he use this for the food or daily need or just for his addiction), and sometimes even the dilemma of whether to give or not to give and if s/he gives to a particular beggar what about others. (Dean 1999)[168]

Regarding the handling of begging issue by welfare states, it can be supposed that the government's aim is to create a society based upon the sense of responsibility towards others. However, government's policies that define begging as a problem of anti-social behaviour, rather than social exclusion and that place an inappropriate emphasis on criminalising begging as a means of tackling this problem could not prove to be fruitful for tackling this issue in long run. Begging is a problem that needs to be dealt urgently as those who are in this situation are caught up in a cycle of poverty and deprivation. However, begging is in itself non-threatening and that where it is accompanied by violent or aggressive behaviour there exist clear means of tackling this (Crisis 2003)[169]. If policies designed to tackle begging are to be effective it is essential that they aim to deal with the root causes of the problem and address the gaps in support and services, enabling and empowering people to escape their plight.

The present study was mainly based on theoretical framework of Oscar Lewis's (1959) theory of the culture of poverty. Lewis's theory of the culture of poverty asserts that poverty as a subculture passes from one generation to another and becomes institutionalized in the poor. According to Lewis, the lack of effective participation and integration in the major institutions of the larger society is one of the crucial characteristics of culture of poverty. The poor (beggars) feel inferiority complex arising out of the dominant values of society regarding accumulation of status, wealth and property. In their childhood children usually absorb the basic values and attitudes of their sub-culture and are not psychologically geared to take full advantage of changing conditions or increased opportunities which may occur in their lifetime. The theory of culture of poverty was very relevant in understanding causes of the begging in present study as many beggars often live in a distinctive sub-culture, which is characterized by poverty, jhuggis, lack of basic facilities etc. They did not actively try to change their situations/conditions (by hardwork and getting formal education) but continued to perpetuate their hereditary sub-culture of beggary and poverty. For most of such beggars, begging is their hereditary occupation or a way of life (their own small world). But it be a mistake to understand beggary in terms of 'culture of poverty' only. There are different other theories and concepts which were helpful in understanding the phenomenon of begging much clearly. Among them the concept of 'Social exclusion' was taken into consideration. The theorists of social exclusion, stress on its multi-dimensional nature. Social exclusion, they argue, relates not simply to a lack of material resources, but also to matters like inadequate social participation, lack of cultural and educational capital, inadequate access to services and lack of power. In other words, the idea of social exclusion attempts to capture the complexity of 'powerlessness' in modern society rather than simply focusing on one of its outcomes. The term social exclusion has also been most generally used to refer to 'persistent and systematic' multiple deprivation (and processes of disempowerment and alienation), as opposed to poverty or disadvantage experienced for short periods of time (Muddiman, 2000).[170] Though, both 'culture of poverty' and 'social exclusion' seems somewhat identical, former (Culture of Poverty) suggests that it is individuals' fault due to which they remain poor and disadvantaged, while latter asserts that it is the system or structure which deprive individuals from basic valuable necessities of life. And again it is the structure of society which has failed to provide them adequate opportunities to uplift them and to bring them in the mainstream society. Thus, social exclusion also helps in great deal to understand the beggary problem in Jammu.

A sample of 50 (10 each from the locations, i.e., religious places, Traffic signals, Bus stands, commercial and shopping hubs and other random places like matadors stands etc.) beggar respondents is selected comprising of both males and females. At few places there were less female beggars than their male counterparts, so available female respondents were chosen from those places. To understand the society's views on beggary, 10 random persons (passer-by near begging places) among the general public were briefly interviewed. They were chosen randomly by purposive sampling technique. Views of individuals on various websites and blogs on topic of begging were also taken into consideration. Therefore, the total sample size for the present study was 60, i.e., 50 beggar respondents and 10 non-beggar respondents.

The present research study has been divided into five chapters including Introduction and Conclusion.

First chapter i.e. '**Introduction**,' has mainly focused on conceptual understanding of begging and review of literature. It has tried to comprehend and explain the begging activity and various research studies on the subject around the world as well as in India. It also discussed the historical context of contemporary begging. It can be concluded from first chapter that begging as an activity of last resort, is not a recent phenomenon but an ancient one, from the earliest known times, although, in earlier times it was much different from the contemporary begging. As suggested by some writers, contemporary begging is mainly a product of the modern capitalist mode of production, where there exists a huge gap between rich and poor (Pande 1986)[171]. The increased number of surplus labour has resulted in many social problem, begging is also one of them.

The second chapter i.e., '**Socio-cultural and Economic profile of Beggars**,' gives a detailed account of beggar's socio-cultural and economic profile, by primarily focusing on such variables like - age, religion, education, place of residence of the respondents, their family and household, their marriage patterns and their economy (daily earning in begging, savings, scarcity) etc. It was observed that most of the beggars who are begging in Jammu city are migrants from other nearby states of India, they belong to different religions, different caste groups and different cultures yet they had similarity due to their engagement in same economic activity, i.e., begging. Most of them were *Hindus* and majority of beggars were illiterate. They had poor housing conditions and mostly live in *Jhuggis*, *kachha* houses or sleep rough on footpaths and other open spaces. The income in begging is also low as compared to other jobs. Most of the beggars said that, in begging, the average daily earning is ` 100 - ` 150 approximately, though a few also claims to earn ` 300 or more daily. Most beggars, also admitted that they were addicted to Tobacco and alcohol.

Third chapter, i.e., '**The Beggary Problem: Reasons of Begging and State's Response**,' has discussed the question "why people beg?" i.e., the reasons of begging. The general reasons listed for begging were destitution, unemployment, illiteracy and lack of skills, disability, hereditary occupation, influence of others, weakness, easy job, isolation, disruptive background, low self-esteem, fun, drugs and alcohol addiction, and also because some of them are on the run. These general reasons of begging could further be categorised into four broad categories (responsible for widespread of begging) - these are Social Exclusion, Culture of poverty, Society's Encouragement and Individual's needs. This chapter has also discussed the legal aspect of begging in reference to anti-begging laws and problems faced by beggars. According to BPBA, 1959, begging is criminalised in 20 states and two union territories including Jammu and Kashmir. J&K has criminalised begging by its own version of anti-begging law (adopted from BPBA, 1959) titled as 'The Jammu and Kashmir, Prevention of Beggary Act, 1960'. According to this Act if one is found guilty, s/he may face imprisonment for 1-10 years.

Fourth chapter, i.e., '**Beggars and Society: Encounters and Techniques**,' has focused on the interactions that take place between beggars and other members of society. This chapter has discussed the stance of society towards begging and beggars, alms giving tradition in various religions and various techniques used by beggars for begging from people. All religions of the world support almsgiving or charity to the poor and needy. However, somehow everywhere people do not like beggars much and also their act of begging is discouraged by society. There are various techniques of begging like active, passive, and aggressive begging. Beggars have to perform different roles in order to get alms. Pity, religious sentiments and physical disability have a prominent role in getting alms and all beggars use these according to their situations. However, many times beggars face harassment from other members of society. They are often condemned for indulging in begging than doing hardwork. They are the victims of social exclusion and stigma.

Fifth chapter, i.e., **'Conclusion,'** deals with the summary and conclusion of the present research study.

MAJOR FINDINGS (INFERENCES) OF THE STUDY

- Begging is a compulsion (not choice) to earn a livelihood and a trap of culture of poverty, contrary to the general assumption which portray begging as an easy job and for lazy and fraud people. Most beggars are poor and needy (right from the time they started begging) but in order to earn more income they may sometimes exaggerate their conditions or try to misrepresent themselves.

- Almost all the beggars were the victims of social exclusion. They have faced exclusion from the prevailing social system and its rights and privileges, typically as a result of poverty or the fact of belonging to a minority social group. They are not considered important in economy, culture and politics of the larger society of which they too are the members. The social exclusion faced by the beggars results in a 'low self-esteem' or 'low self-regard' among them. So, they do not see begging so much demeaning activity as seen by majority society. As it is mainly self-esteem which stops people from begging (otherwise most people would have been beggars), so, with a low self-esteem, it is not much difficult for them to start begging.

- As per Census of India beggars are non-workers, and begging is not considered as work but individuals involved in begging see it as a work. For them although it is of low level work but still it is a work which can generate them some income. And, no matter whether they like or dislike begging, it was only begging which helped them survive during the worst phase of their life.

- Most of the beggars were above 30 years of age (excluding child beggars, which are not part of present research). While most males were concentrated between age group of 51-70, and most females were in age group of 31-50 years. This indicates that they usually start begging at a later stage of life mostly when they face prolonged poverty and unemployment. Some beggars started begging at later stage of life because they were physically unable to do any other work and had no one to support them financially.

- Most of the beggar respondents in Jammu were Hindus (64%) but there were also a significant number of Muslim beggars (30%). It can be noted that Jammu is known as a city of temples and have majority population of Hindus which can be the reason of more Hindu beggars here.

- Most of the beggar respondents, in the present study, were illiterate. Lack of education was prominent among them due to which they remained unemployable and unmotivated for any progress or mobility. Due to illiteracy they also lacked skills that are needed for employment in modern world where unskilled (and uneducated) persons are unfit for any work except manual labour.

- Among the beggar respondents only six (12%) were local beggars while other were from different states of India which includes Chhattisgarh (14%), Rajasthan (14%), Uttar Pradesh (12%), Madhya Pradesh (10%), Bihar (8%), Maharashtra (4%), Punjab (4%), Haryana (4%) and Jharkhand (4%). While five beggars (14%) didn't reply to this question. Some migrant beggars responded that they are in J&K from last almost 30 to 50 years and permanently left their native states as they had no land there, while many others said that they were in this city from roughly around last 1 to 10 years.

- During the study, it was found that beggars were mostly living in *Jhuggis* (48%) or *Kachha* houses (12%) or have no shelter (26%). In Jammu, they mainly resided in the areas like- Belicharana, Rani Bagh, Vijaypur, Marathi Mohalla Trikuta Nagar, Raje Chak Akhnoor, Bage-e-Bahu, Raghunath Market, Railway Station, Bohri Talab Tillo, Kanpuria Basti Rajiv Nagar Narwal, Empty

Space under Fly Over, Bus Stand JDA complex, Panjtirthi, Muthi Gaon National Highway Nagrota, Thandi Khui, Mishriwala etc.

- Most of the beggars (70%) followed a migratory, or rotation pattern. Only 30% beggar respondents said that they beg at on fixed place. Though some beggars sit at one particular place for begging, most of them beg at different places on the different days of the week, i.e., they follow rotation technique. Some beggars also migrate to other places, especially to Kashmir region due to hot summer in Jammu. As most of the beggar in Jammu city are migrated from other states of India they can migrate to other states when they face some serious problems here.

- Most of the beggar respondents (56%) had nuclear family but before coming into begging majority of them had joint families. Therefore, the data clearly indicates that begging has led to nuclearisation of families.

- Majority of the beggar respondents said that they had approximately about 1-4 dependents at home for whom they have to earn adequately. But 40% of the total respondents admitted that they earn for themselves as they had no dependents on them.

- It was found that there was not any significant difference in number of beggars on the basis of their marital status but when one observes the marital status on the basis of gender, most of the men (45%) beggar respondents were married while women (57%) respondents in begging were mostly widows.

- Most beggar (60%) respondents said that they take only two meals daily while 40% beggars take three meals daily. In Jammu, beggars mostly get at least one meal as alms from others. The free meal could be given by some individuals or leftovers from dhaba (small roadside food points) or *langer/bhandara* (a kind of feast) in temple. Among total 50 respondents, 28 (56%) beggars said that they were vegetarian while 22 (44%) acknowledged that though they mostly take vegetarian food, sometime they also take non-vegetarian food (mostly chicken or eggs).

- Addiction was common among beggars. Only 10% beggars said that they were not addicted to any tobacco product or alcohol. 18% beggars said that they only take tobacco product (like *Beedi*, *Kheni* etc.), a majority i.e., 62% beggars said that they were addicted to both Tobacco products and Alcohol (mostly desi whisky pouch commonly known as *'Frooti'*). Tobacco is used as daily addiction while alcohol consumption varies from beggar to beggar. Some may consume it on daily basis and others occasionally. However, from these figures one cannot draw the conclusion that beggars are mostly alcoholic and beg to support their addiction. If we look at alcohol consumption pattern of other people in Jammu city we may find these figure normal as alcohol consumption is becoming a cultural habit among poor, middle class and equally among rich.

- Most beggars said that the daily income is low in begging. They earn about ` 100 daily (as per beggar's accounts) , though some of them also earn about ` 300 or more, which shows that begging is not a much profitable as compared to other jobs for similar skills level like that of manual labourers whose daily income is more than ` 300. The able-bodied beggars, preferred begging over manual labour work mainly because in begging one can get instant money and without waiting for or getting cheated from the contractors or other middlemen.

- 24% beggars said that they were not satisfied with their income as it became very tough for them to meet all the expenses of daily life. However, 40% beggars said that they were somewhat satisfied and 36% beggars said that they were fully satisfied with their daily earnings, these were the ones who earn good enough money or have other earning members (sources) in the family.

- 84% beggar respondents said that they have no other source of income other than begging while 16% said that they have other source too like land in their village etc. Those who save money said that they even have bank accounts where they can save without any threat of being stolen or cheating.

- Most of the respondents in Jammu city were in begging from past 5-15 years and majority of them said that they started begging almost after attaining the age of thirty years or more.

- The occupation of the parents (in majority cases refers to father) of 24% beggars were farming or farm labourer, while 20% were labourers, 16% were beggars, one was Barber, 6% were sweepers, 4% were in some government jobs (contractual), while one said that his father was priest in a temple. Thus, except a few, parental occupation of most of the respondents falls in lower class in modern societies. The one whose parents were in Government job, were engaged in class IVth jobs (like peon etc.) and were no more with them (died). The data also signifies that beggars did not belong to lower class strata only (like poverty) but were spread across different castes.

- In the present study, 26% respondents said that they had directly started begging without doing any other work. However, the remaining respondents said that they were in some other works/occupations or jobs before coming into begging. 32% said that they were labourers prior to joining begging, 10% were kabaddis, six 12% were agricultural labourers, and so on. Majority of the respondents were either labourer or had no work before coming into begging.

- Most of the beggar (62%) respondents said that they save their money for future as there exists uncertainty over when there arises a need for money.

- There is no single reason for begging. People beg for different reasons, for multiple reasons concurrently. The main reasons of begging were destitution, hereditary occupation, Turmoil in life, religious tradition of alms-giving, unemployment, low self-esteem, illiteracy and lack of skills etc. If one view begging from broad perspective, the reasons of begging can be categorised as Social exclusion, Culture of poverty, Society's encouragement, and Individual's needs.

- Religious factors such as zakat in Muslims and Daana in Hinduism serve to socially and financially legitimize beggary.

Beggars take advantage of this and use religion as a tool in begging. Most of the respondents agreed that very often they use religious sentiments to beg from people. During the study it was also found that the beggars, irrespective of their religion, were found begging at different religious places (and not restricted to their own religious places). Some beggars also used different attires during different days to beg (as they considered this as a technique to get more alms and earn more). In Hindu philosophy, there are different days which are meant for specific God and Goddess, they too catch up with myth, like carrying a photograph of *'Mata Rani'* and *'Lord Hanuman'* on Tuesday, carrying idol of *'Lord Shiva'* on Monday and there are so many beggars who can be seen coming door to door especially on Saturday carrying an idol of *'Shani Dev'* to beg alms. Beggars also adopt the other religious or social ethos as required in a particular setting to make an emotional (also spiritual) appeal to the passer-by. But one of the limitation, the researcher was not able to overcome, was that the beggars who use this as a technique did not reveal their (real) religion.

- People dislike beggars mainly because of the fact that many able bodied persons are in begging who could otherwise do some other work. They usually view them as frauds. People also see them as unwanted migrants and parasites on the existing resources as they do not contribute but remain dependent only. They are also disliked for being migrants, causing nuisance to the locals and making cities look ugly (allegedly spoils beautification of the city) with their unhygienic lifestyle.

- Many beggars were ready to leave begging, only if they are provided with some alternate job where they can earn equivalent or more than what they get in begging. However once one gets into begging, it is not easy for him/her to leave it as they become habitual to it and no more afraid of the stigma attached to it.

- Government is not bothered to genuinely help this class. It only made a law regarding the beggars and that too to criminalise them. The problem here is that governmental authorities view begging as 'deviant-behaviour problem' instead of a problem of social exclusion. As they view begging as a sort of crime and thus try to curb it like other crimes. Even if this may be the case, still the anti-beggary laws are not implemented properly, which means beggary is not a subject of interest for the government and they don't want to use its resources on it.

- Last but not least, there is a general assumption among the public that begging activity is operated by some gangs [as during the study whomever the researcher told that he is researching begging, they have a special advice for him, 'Oh! You know, there are many gangs and rackets of these beggars...]. Various reports in media have spreaded this rumour (seems so in most of the cases and also in context of present study) about beggar gangs and begging mafia. It is rumoured that these gangs use beggars, especially children (many of whom are deformed by these mafia gangs), to earn huge amount of money. Malik (2012),[172] asserted that, to verify such reports, the Delhi Police was asked by the Delhi High Court to investigate allegations of such mafias, and it finally reported on oath to the court that the Delhi Crime Branch has found no evidence of such mafias. This indicates that either there is a nexus between the policemen and the gangs, who finds it better to keep schtum about it or that there is no mafia involvement. In present study also, no such gangs were found to be operating in Jammu city and even they (beggars) do not give '*hafta*' to police or any such person. But there are some *Deras* (as discussed in chapter II) or groups of few begging families, who, though, work independently may support one another during exigencies like fight with other groups etc.

Begging is a social problem as it is against the societal norm that stresses on, 'one should earn his own livelihood by hardwork and not to be an parasite on others' and also because the number of beggars has increased to an alarming extent. Beggars are blamed for causing nuisance and spreading diseases due to their unhygienic life style. But, they are also humans, who due to some circumstances are into the begging activity. Coming to the societal norm, though it is upheld by majority of the society but some have failed due to certain reasons like, what if one is unable to earn one's livelihood and has no one to support him/her financially? S/he has left with no other option but to beg. However the beggary problem is not because of beggars alone, as begging is a process of interaction between beggars and society. Values in a social system (especially in Religion) encourages people to donate which indirectly encourages some people to beg. It is very difficult to curb beggary completely (as there still exist beggars in developed western countries) but it can be reduced to normal state with efforts from all the three sides (or stakeholders) Government, Society, and Beggars. In the study, one finds the existence of different type of beggars in Jammu city and different reasons (the beggars give) for their begging activity. From the study, it is, therefore, concluded that beggars are the marginals within the marginalised community. Culture of poverty persist among them and they are also socially excluded from the mainstream (society).

NOTES

[167] Madhav Sadashiv Gore. 1958. "Society and the Beggar." *Sociological Bulletin* 7 (1): 23-48. Accessed September 30, 2015. http://www.jstor.org/stable/42864528.

[168] Hartley Dean, ed. 1999. *Begging Questions: Street-level economic activity and social policy failure*. Bristol: The Policy Press.

[169] Crisis. 2003. "Begging & Anti-Social Behaviour." *Crisis: The national charity for homeless people*. April 4. Accessed January 17, 2016. http://www.crisis.org.uk/data/files/publications/AntiSoc_response%5B1%5D.pdf.

[170] Dave Muddiman. 2000. "Theories of social exclusion and the public library." In *Open to All?: the Public Library and Social Exclusion*, by Dave Muddiman, 1-15. London: The Council for Museums, Archives and Libraries.

[171] B.B Pande. 1986. "Rights of Beggars and Vagrants." *India International Centre Quarterly* 13 (4): 115-132. Accessed October 16, 2015. http://www.jstor.org/stable/23001440.

[172] Mehak Malik. 2012. *Street Begging in Delhi: A Study of Anti-Begging Act and Institutional Arrangements for Homeless People*. Working Paper, New Delhi: Centre for Civil Society

BIBLIOGRAPHY

- Abebe, Tatek. 2009. "Begging as a Livelihood Pathway of Street Children in Addis Ababa." *Forum for Development Studies* 36 (2): 275-300. doi:10.1080/08039410.2009.9666438.

- Abercrombie, Nicholas, Stephen Hill, and Bryan S. Turner. 1984. *The Penguin Dictionary of Sociology.* London: Penguin Books.

- Acharya, Subrata Kumar. 1988. "Evolution of The Institution of Beggary in Ancient India." *Annals of the Bhandarkar Oriental Research Institute* 69 (1): 269-277. Accessed September 30, 2015. http://www.jstor.org/stable/41693775.

- Ahmadi, H. 2010. "A Study of Beggar Characteristics and Attitude of People Towards the Phenomenon of Begging in The City of Shiraz." *Journal of Applied Sociology* 39 (3): 135-148. Accessed January 7, 2016. http://www.sid.ir/en/VEWSSID/J_pdf/128520103908.pdf.

- 2016. *Begging for Life- From Manila to Malmo (Documentary).* Directed by Barnaby Phillips and Karim Shah. Performed by Al Jazeera English. Accessed August 23, 2016. http://www.aljazeera.com/programmes/peopleandpower/2016/01/begging-life-160126130424263.html.

- Anderson, Nels. 1961. *The Hobo: The sociology of the homeless man*. The University of Chicago: Phoenix Books.

- Baker, Dennis J. 2009. "A Critical Evaluation of the Historical and Contemporary Justifications for Criminalising Begging." *The Journal of Criminal Law* 48 (1): 212-240. doi:10.1177/0042098009360688.

- Bardach, Eugene, and Eric M. Patashnik. 2006. *A Practical Guide for Policy Analysis: The Eightfold Path to More Effective Problem Solving*. 5th. Washington DC: CQ Press.

- Becker, Howard Saul. 1963. *Outsiders: Studies in the Sociology of Deviance*. New York: The Free Press.

- Benthall, Jonathan. 1999. "Financial Worship: The Quranic Injunction to Almsgiving." *The Journal of the Royal Anthropological Institute* 5 (1): 27-42. doi:10.2307/2660961.

- Berger, Peter L. 1963. *Invitation to Sociology: A Humanistic Perspective*. New York: Doubleday & Co.

- Bromley, Ray. 1981. "Begging in Cali: Image, Reality and Policy." *International Social Work* 24 (2): 22-40. doi:10.1177/002087288102400205.

- Bruce, Steve, and Steven Yearley. 2006. *The Sage Dictionary of Sociology*. London: SAGE Publications.

- Butovskaya, M., F. Salter, I. Diakonov, and A. Smirnov. 2000. "Urban Begging and Ethnic Nepotism in Russia: An Ethological Pilot Study." *Human Nature* 11 (2): 157-182. doi:10.1007/s12110-000-1017-z.

- Charlesworth, Lorie. 1999. "Why Is It A Crime To Be Poor?" *Liverpool Law Review* 21 (2): 149–167. doi:10.1023/A:1005686302457.

- Collective for Social Science Research, Karachi. 2004. *A rapid assessment of bonded labour in domestic work and begging in Pakistan*. Working Paper, Geneva: International Labour Office. Accessed October 4, 2015.

http://www.ilo.org/wcmsp5/groups/public/@ed_norm/@declar ation/documents/publication/wcms_082030.pdf.

- Cook, S. "India Beggars and Begging Scams: What You Should Know." *About Travel (about.com).* Accessed July 2, 2016. http://goindia.about.com/od/annoyancesinconveniences/p/india begging.htm.

- Crisis. 2003. "Begging & Anti-Social Behaviour." *Crisis: The national charity for homeless people.* April 4. Accessed January 17, 2016. http://www.crisis.org.uk/data/files/publications/AntiSoc_respons e%5B1%5D.pdf.

- Dean, Hartley, ed. 1999. *Begging Questions: Street-level economic activity and social policy failure.* Bristol: The Policy Press.

- Dean, Hartley, and Margaret Melrose. 1999. "Easy pickings or hard profession? Begging as an economic activity." In *Begging Questions: Street-level economic activity and social policy failure*, edited by Hartley Dean, 83-100. Bristol: The Policy Press.

- Delap, Emily. 2009. *Begging for Change.* London: Anti-Slavery International.

- "Dharma Data: Nirvana." *Buddhanet.* Accessed July 11, 2016. http://www.buddhanet.net/e-learning/dharmadata/fdd43.htm.

- Dromi, Shai M. 2012. "Penny for Your Thoughts: Beggars and the Exercise of Morality in Daily Life." *Sociological Forum* 27 (4): 847-871. doi:10.1111/j.1573-7861.2012.01359.x.

- Erskine, Angus, and Ian McIntosh. 1999. "Why begging offends: historical perspectives and continuities." In *Begging Questions: Street-level economic activity and social policy failure*, edited by Hartley Dean, 27-42. Bristol: The Policy Press.

- Ferguson, Christopher. 2015. "The Political Economy of the Street and its Discontents." *Cultural and Social History* 12 (1): 27-50. doi:10.2752/147800415X14135484867108.

- Foltz, Franz, and Frederick Foltz. 2010. "Charity in a Technological Society: From Alms to Corporation." *Bulletin of*

Science, Technology & Society 30 (2): 96-102.
doi:10.1177/0270467610365165.

- Foucault, Michel. 1977. *Discipline and Punish: The Birth of the Prison.*
New York City: Pantheon Books.

- Frink, Sandra. 2010. "Strangers are Flocking Here: Identity and
Anonymity in New Orleans, 1810-1860." *American Nineteenth
Century History* 11 (2): 155-181. doi:10.1080/14664658.2010.481869.

- Gay, Paul du, and Michael Pryke. 2002. *Cultural Economy: Cultural
analysis and commercial life.* London: Sage Publication.

- Gill, Flora. 1999. "The meaning of work Lessons from sociology,
psychology, and political theory." *Journal of Socio-Economics* 28 (6):
725-743. doi:10.1016/S1053-5357(99)00054-2.

- Gillin, J. L. 1929. "Vagrancy and Begging." *American Journal of
Sociology* 35 (3): 424-432. Accessed May 21, 2016.
http://www.jstor.org/stable/2765752.

- 2013. "Global employment trends 2013." *International Labour
Organization.* January 21. Accessed December 29, 2015.
(http://www.ilo.org/wcmsp5/groups/public/---dgreports/---
dcomm/---publ/documents/publication/wcms_202326.pdf.

- Goffman, Erving. 1953. *Communication Conduct in an Island
Community.* PhD Thesis, University of Chicago.

- Gore, M.S., J.S. Mathur, M.R. Laljani, and H.S Takulia. 1959. *The
Beggar Problem in Metropolitan Delhi.* Delhi: School of Social Work.

- Gore, Madhav Sadashiv. 1958. "Society and the Beggar." *Sociological
Bulletin* 7 (1): 23-48. Accessed September 30, 2015.
http://www.jstor.org/stable/42864528.

- *Greater Kashmir.* 2016. "Liquor consumption increases in J&K."
June 1. Accessed June 2, 2016.
http://www.greaterkashmir.com/news/kashmir/liquor-
consumption-increases-in-j-k/219154.html.

- Hagan, John, and Bill McCarthy. 1998. *Mean Streets: Youth Crime and
Homelessness.* Cambridge: Cambridge University Press. 1998.

- Hayati, A. Majid, and Mahmood Maniati. 2010. "Beggars are sometimes the choosers!" *Discourse & Society* 21 (1): 41–57. doi:10.1177/0957926509345069.

- Heim, Maria. 2004. *Theories of the gift in South Asia: Hindu, Buddhist, and Jain reflections on Dana.* New York: Routledge.

- Hermer, J. 1999. *Policing Compassion: begging, law and power in public places,.* Ph.D. Thesis, University of Oxford.

- Hodson, Randy, and Teresa A. Sullivan. 2012. *The Social Organization of Work.* Belmont, CA: Cengage Learning.

- —. 2008. *The Social Organization of Work.* Belmont: Thomson Wadsworth.

- Horn, Michael, and Michelle Cooke. 2011. *A Question Of Begging: A study of the extent and nature of begging in the City of Melbourne.* Research Study, Melbourne: Hanover.

- ICCR. "Charity." *Islamic Center of Cedar Rapids.* Accessed June 12, 2016. http://crmosque.com/islam-l0l/charity-zakah.

- International Encyclopedia of the Social Sciences. 2008. "Culture of Poverty." *Encyclopedia.com.* Accessed May 6, 206. http://www.encyclopedia.com/social-sciences/applied-and-social-sciences-magazines/culture-poverty.

- Jha, M. 1979. *The Beggars of a pilgrim's city: anthropological, sociological, historical & religious aspects of beggars and lepers of Puri.* Varanasi: Kishor Vidya Niketan.

- Johansson, Rune Edvin A. 1970. *The Psychology of Nirvana.* New York: Doubleday & Company Inc.

- Jonsson, David. 2006. *Islamic Economics and the Final Jihad: The Muslim Brotherhood to the Leftist/Marxist - Islamist Alliance.* California: Xulon Press.

- Jordan, Bill. 1999. "Begging: the global context and international comparisons." In *Begging Questions: Street-level economic activity and social policy failure,* edited by Hartley Dean, 43-62. Bristol: The policy Press.

- Jupp, Victor, ed. 2006. *The Sage Dictionary of Social Research Methods*. London: SAGE Publications.

- Jütfe, Robert. 1981. "Poor Relief and Social Discipline in Sixteenth-Century Europe." *European History Quarterly* 11 (1): 25-52. doi:10.1177/026569148101100102.

- Kamat, K.L. 1997. "The Begging Profession." *Kamat's Potpourri*. August 15. Accessed May 24, 2016. http://www.kamat.com/kalranga/bhiksha/begging.htm.

- Kassah, Alexander Kwesi. 2008. "Begging as work: a study of people with mobility difficulties in Accra, Ghana." *Disability & Society* 23 (2): 163-170. doi:10.1080/09687590701841208.

- Kennedy, Catherine, and Suzanne Fitzpatrick. 2001. "Begging, Rough Sleeping and Social Exclusion: Implications for Social Policy." *Urban Studies* 30 (11): 2001-2016. doi:10.1080/00420980120080907.

- Khan, Jabir Hasan, Menka, and Shamshad. 2013. "Problems of Beggars: A Case Study." *International Journal of Management and Social Sciences Research (IJMSSR)* 67-74. Accessed March 11, 2016. http://www.irjcjournals.org/ijmssr/Dec2013/11.pdf.

- Kochuyt, Thierry. 2009. "God, Gifts and Poor People: On Charity in Islam." *Social Compass* 56 (1): 98–116. doi:10.1177/0037768608100345.

- Kumarappa, J.M., ed. 1945. *Our Beggar Problem: How to tackle it*. Bombay: Padma Publication Ltd.

- Lankenau, Stephen E. 1999. "Panhandling repertoires and routines for overcoming the nonperson treatment." *Deviant Behaviour* 20 (2): 183-206. doi:10.1080/016396299266551.

- Levi-Strauss, Claude. 1974. *Structural Anthropology*. New York: Basic Books.

- Lewis, Oscar. 1969. *A Death In The Sanchez Family*. New York: Penguin Books Ltd.

- Lewis, Oscar. 1959. *Five Families: Mexican Case Studies in the Culture of Poverty*. New York: Basic Books.

- Lewis, Oscar. 1998. "The Culture of Poverty." *Society* 35 (2): 7-30. doi:10.1007/BF02838122.

- Lewis, Oscar. 1963. "The Culture of Poverty." *Society* 1 (1): 17-19. doi:10.1007/BF03182237.

- Lipkin, Zwia. 2005. "Modern Dilemmas: Dealing with Nanjing's Beggars, 1927-1937." *Journal of Urban History* 31 (5): 583-609. doi:10.1177/0096144205275730.

- Lu, Hanchao. 1999. "Becoming Urban: Mendicancy and Vagrants in Modern Shanghai." *Journal of Social History* 33 (1): 7-36. Accessed December 24, 2015. http://www.jstor.org/stable/3789458.

- Mack, Joanna. 2016. "Social exclusion." *Poverty*. January 21. Accessed June 2016, 17. http://www.poverty.ac.uk/definitions-poverty/social-exclusion.

- Malik, Mehak. 2012. *Street Begging in Delhi: A Study of Anti-Begging Act and Institutional Arrangements for Homeless People*. Working Paper, New Delhi: Centre for Civil Society.

- Malik, Sonia, and Sanjoy Roy. 2012. "A Study on Begging: A Social Stigma-An Indian Perspective." *Journal of Human Values* 18 (2): 187-199. doi:10.1177/0971685812454486.

- Mansour, Essam. 2015. "An explanatory study into the information seeking-behaviour of Egyptian beggars." *Journal of Librarianship and Information Science* 1-16. doi:10.1177/0961000615622679.

- Marx, Karl. 1867. *Capital: A Critique of Political Economy*. Edited by Frederick Engels. Translated by Samuel Moore and Edward Aveling. Vol. I. Moscow: Progress Publishers. Accessed October 21, 2015. https://www.marxists.org/archive/marx/works/1867-c1/.

- Marx, Karl. 1863. *Capital: Theories of Surplus Value*. Vol. IV. Moscow: Progress Publishers. Accessed October 29, 2014.

https://www.marxists.org/archive/marx/works/1863/theories-surplus-value/.

- Marx, Karl. 1843. *Critique of Hegel's Philosophy of Right.* Translated by Annette Jolin and Joseph O'Malley. Cambridge: Cambridge University Press. Accessed May 06, 2015. https://www.marxists.org/archive/marx/works/1843/critique-hpr/index.htm.

- Mathieson, Jane, Jennie Popay, Etheline Enoch, Sarah Escorel, Mario Hernandez, Heidi Johnston, and Laetitia Rispe. 2008. *Social Exclusion: Meaning, measurement and experience and links to health inequalities - A review of literature.* Background Paper, WHO. Accessed June 9, 2016. http://www.who.int/social_determinants/media/sekn_meaning_measurement_experience_2008.pdf.pdf.

- McIntosh, Ian, and Angus Erskine. 2000. "Money for nothing?: Understanding Giving to Beggars." *Sociological Research Online* 5 (1). Accessed March 19, 2016. http://www.socresonline.org.uk/5/1/mcintosh.html.

- Melrose, Margaret. 1999. "Word From the Street: Perils and Pains of Researching Begging." In *Begging Questions: Street-level Economic Activity and Social Policy Failure,* by Hartley Dean, 143-161. Bristol: The Policy Press.

- Mills, C. Wright. 1959. *The Sociological Imagination.* New York: Oxford University Press.

- Ministry of Social Justice & Empowerment, GOI. 2016. *Press Information Bureau.* Accessed June 11, 2016. http://pib.nic.in/newsite/PrintR.elease.aspx?relid=67734.

- Moorthy, M.Vasudeva. 1959. *Beggar Problem in Greater Bombay: A Research Study.* A Research Study, Bombay: Indian Conference of Social Work.

- Muddiman, Dave. 2000. "Theories of social exclusion and the public library." In *Open to All? : the Public Library and Social Exclusion,* by Dave Muddiman, 1-15. London: The Council for Museums, Archives and Libraries.

- Mukherjee, Dyutimoy. 2008. "Laws For Beggars, Justice for Whom: A Critical Review of the Bombay Prevention of Begging Act 1959." *The International Journal of Human Rights* 12 (2): 279-288. doi:10.1080/13642980801899709.

- Muñoz, Cristian Pérez, and Joshua D Potter. 2013. "Street-level charity: Beggars, donors, and welfare policies." *Journal of Theoretical Politics* 26 (1): 158-174. doi:10.1177/0951629813493836.

- Murdoch, Alison, Liz Connell, Jean Davis, and Joanne Maher. 1994. *We are human too: a study of people who beg.* London: Crisis.

- Namwata, Baltazar M.L., and Maseke R. Mgabo. 2012. "Feelings of Beggars on Begging Life and their Survival Livelihoods in Urban Areas of Central Tanzania." *International Journal of Physical and Social Sciences (IJPSS)* 2 (7). Accessed December 20, 2015. http://www.ijmra.us/project%20doc/IJPSS_JULY2012/IJMRA-PSS1401.pdf.

- NSID. 2014. "Beggary Prevention." *National Institute of Social Defence.* Accessed June 16, 2016. http://www.nisd.gov.in/content/213_3_BeggaryPrevention.aspx.

- Orwell, George. 1933. *Down and out in Paris and London.* London: Victor Gollancz. Quoted by Dean 1999.

- Pande, B.B. 1986. "Rights of Beggars and Vagrants." *India International Centre Quarterly* 13 (4): 115-132. Accessed October 16, 2015. http://www.jstor.org/stable/23001440.

- Parsons, Talcott. 1951. *The Social System.* London: Routledge & Kegan Paul Ltd.

- Patel, Tara. 1959. "Some Reflections of the Beggar Problem in Ahmedabad." *Sociological Bulletin* 8 (1): 5-15. Accessed September 30, 2015. http://www.jstor.org/stable/42864545.

- Pion, Georgine M., and David S. Cordray. "Research Methods." *Encyclopedia of Education.* Accessed December 18, 2015. http://www.encyclopedia.com.

- "Poverty." *merriam-webster.* Accessed June 18, 2016. http://www.merriam-webster.com/dictionary/poverty.

- Prabhupada, A.C. Bhaktivedanta Swami. 1983. *Bhagvad Gita - As it is.* California: Bhaktivedanta Book Trust International.

- PTI. 2015. "Over 4 lakh beggars in India, most in West Bengal: Govt." *The Indian Express,* August 13. Accessed January 15, 2016. http://indianexpress.com/article/india/india-others/over-4-lakh-beggars-in-india-most-in-west-bengal-govt/.

- Puri, Sanjay. 2015. "Begging in Jammu, a work not compulsion." *State Times,* July 22. Accessed November 4, 2015. http://news.statetimes.in/begging-in-jammu-a-work-not-compulsion/.

- Rafiuddin, Mohd. 2008. *Beggars in Hyderabad: A Study on Understanding the Economics of Beggary in Hyderabad - an Insight Into Rehabilitation Possibilities.* Begaluru: Books for Change.

- Raj, Pushkar. 2005. *Criminalising poverty: Houseless and anti-beggary law in Delhi.* New Delhi: PUCL Bulletin. Accessed January 30, 2016. http://www.pucl.org/Topics/Industries-envirn-resettlement/2004/criminalise-poverty.htm.

- Ramanathan, Usha. 2008. "Ostensible Poverty, Beggary and the Law." *Economic and Political Weekly* 43 (44): 33, 35-44. Accessed September 30, 2015. http://www.jstor.org/stable/40278127.

- Rao, Amiya. 1981. "Poverty and Power: The Anti-Begging Act." *Economic and Political Weekly* 16 (8): 269-270. Accessed February 02, 2016. http://www.jstor.org/stable/4369560.

- Rao, Amiya, Sunil Battacharya, and Aurobindo Ghose. *A Report on Begging in Delhi.* PUCL.

- Registrar General and Census Commision. "Concepts and Definitions." *Census of India.* Accessed June 11, 2016.

http://censusindia.gov.in/Data_Products/Data_Highlights/Data_Highlights_link/concepts_def_hh.pdf.

- Saeed, Sheba. 2013. *Regulation of Begging in Mumbai: A Critique of Religious and Secular Laws and Notions of Power.* University of Birmingham: Ph.D. Thesis.

- Saeed, Sheba. 2014. *The Business of Begging.* August 31. https://www.foreignaffairs.com/articles/india/2014-08-31/business-begging.

- Scanlon, Edward. 2005. "Critical Perspectives on Welfare and Poverty: A Review Essay of Regulating the Poor and Flat Broke ." *Qualitative Social Work* 4 (1): 114-122. doi:10.1177/1473325005050210.

- Sen, Amartya. 2000. *Social Exclusion: Concept, Application, and Scrutiny.* Manila: Asian Development Bank.

- Shichor, David, and Ruth Ellis. 1981. "Begging in Israel: An exploratory study." *Deviant Behavior* 2 (2): 109-125. doi:10.1080/01639625.1981.9967546.

- Stead, Sergeant Ian, and Cheshire Constabulary. 2010. "Begging." *Politics.co.uk.* Accessed October 10, 2015. http://www.politics.co.uk/reference/begging.

- Stein, Burton. 1960. "The Economic Function of a Medieval South Indian Temple." *The Journal of Asian Studies* 19 (2): 163-76. doi:10.2307/2943547.

- Stones, Christopher R. 2013. "A psycho-social exploration of street begging: A qualitative study." *South African Journal of Psychology* 43 (2): 157-166. doi:10.1177/0081246313482632.

- Thakker Y., Gandhi Z., Sheth H., Vankar G.K., & Shroff S. 2007. "Psychiatry Morbidity Among Inmates of the 'Beggar Home'." *International Journal of Psychosocial Rehabilitation* 11 (2): 31-36. Accessed September 30, 2015. http://www.psychosocial.com/IJPR_11/Illness_in_Beggars_Home_Sheth.html.

- Thapar, Romila. 1981. "The householder and the renouncer in the Brahmanical and Buddhist traditions." *Contributions to Indian Sociology* 15 (1): 273-298. doi:10.1177/006996678101500115.

- *The Times of India.* 2016. "A dream shattered: Cops find starlet begging and stealing." April 26. Accessed November 4, 2015. http://timesofindia.indiatimes.com/city/mumbai/A-dream-shattered-Cops-find-starlet-begging-and-stealing/articleshow/51988079.cms.

- *The Times of India.* 2016. "Activist 'begs' to protest government's failure of school schemes." July 1. Accessed July 13, 2016. http://timesofindia.indiatimes.com/city/coimbatore/Activist-begs-to-protest-govt-failure-of-school-schemes/articleshow/53001320.cms?from=mdr.

- *The Times of India.* 2016. "Doctors take out march with begging bowls." February 3. Accessed March 4, 2016. http://timesofindia.indiatimes.com/city/delhi/Doctors-take-out-march-with-begging-bowls/articleshow/50827751.cms.

- *The Times of India.* 2007. "Gita's story: From ramp model to beggar." September 4. Accessed November 4, 2015. http://timesofindia.indiatimes.com/india/Gitas-story-From-ramp-model-to-beggar/articleshow/2335845.cms.

- *The Times of India.* 2016. "Parents go 'begging' to protest steep school fees." April 5. Accessed April 8, 2016. http://timesofindia.indiatimes.com/city/ludhiana/Parents-go-begging-to-protest-steep-school-fees/articleshow/51705017.cms.

- Turner, Bryan S. 2006. *The Cambridge Dictionary of Sociology.* New York: Cambridge University Press.

- Turner, C. J. R. 1887. *A History Vagrants & Vargancy And Beggars & Begging.* London: Chapman and Hall Ltd.

- UNDP. "Millennium Development Goals Indicators." *The official United Nations site for the MDG Indicators.* Accessed August 21, 2015. http://mdgs.un.org/unsd/mdg/Metadata.aspx?IndicatorId=0&SeriesId=597.

- UNESCO. 2004. *The Plurality of Literacy and its implications for Policies and Programs*. Position Paper, Paris: United Nations Educational, Scientific and Cultural Organization. Accessed January 13, 2016. http://unesdoc.unesco.org/images/0013/001362/136246e.pdf.

- Wardhaugh, Julia. 2009. "Regulating social space: Begging in two South Asian Cities." *Crime Media Culture* 5 (3): 333-341. doi:10.1177/1741659009346020.

- WHO. "Disabilities." *World Health Organization*. Accessed May 17, 2016. http://www.who.int/topics/disabilities/en/.

- Wikipedia contributors. "Alms." *Wikipedia, The Free Encyclopedia*. Accessed June 14, 2016. https://en.wikipedia.org/wiki/Alms.

- —. "Culture of poverty." *Wikipedia, The Free Encyclopedia*. Accessed June 21, 2016. https://en.wikipedia.org/w/index.php?title=Culture_of_poverty&oldid=738439201.

- —. "Vagrancy (people)." *Wikipedia, The Free Encyclopedia*. Accessed March 16, 2016. https://en.wikipedia.org/w/index.php?title=Vagrancy_(people)&oldid=741149179.

ABOUT THE AUTHOR

Bachitter Singh is a research scholar in Sociology from Jammu, J&K (India). He has Qualified UGC NET-JRF (Junior Research Fellowship) and SET in Sociology.

Contact Author at: manhasju@hotmail.com / manhas219@gmail.com